Journey

with Me:
Getting to Know

God

Marlene Libby

ISBN 978-1-68570-531-2 (paperback)
ISBN 978-1-68570-532-9 (digital)

Christian Faith Publishing
832 Park Avenue
Meadville, PA 16335
www.christianfaithpublishing.com

Printed in the United States of America

To our sons and daughters, whom we are extremely proud of, Sue, Ned, Robbin, Mark, Todd, and Troy, and our grandchildren and great-grandchildren, as a legacy from an amazing man.

In memory of William "Bill" H. Libby

Born in Winona, Minnesota, he attended Carleton College and took up organic chemistry. In World War II, he was a First LT-USAF B-17 pilot with nineteen missions. He received his PhD in organic chemistry at the University of Illinois. He was employed by Fortune 500 company in Saint Paul, Minnesota, as a chemist. He retired as marketing director in the engineering systems and interred with military honors at Fort Snelling, Minnesota.

Bill was interviewed about his years of service in World War II one month before he passed away. It has been accepted and is on file at the Library of Congress, along with documents and photographs. He wrote notes about all of his nineteen missions.

Bill was a devout Christian who found lifelong peace and comfort in his faith. He enjoyed playing golf, working puzzles, reading books, cooking, writing articles, and traveling both the United States and worldwide.

Bill's company was enjoyed by all ages. A recent honor to him was by his nine-year-old great-grandson, Damien, who was asked to write about "his hero." He picked his great-grandpa stating, "My hero is my great-grandpa. He was in World War II and in the military and I love him." Bill played games with several great-grandchildren from around the country two weeks before his death. He was able to meet and lay a hand on his youngest great-grandson, Grayson.

The most frequent used adjective in describing Bill was "amazing." That he was!

Contents

Acknowledgment

I am so grateful and blessed by God to have had the encouragement and expertise available to me in preparing this manuscript. To my grandson Tyler, my computer/technology expert who had unbelievable patience with his grandmother. To my longtime friend, Nora, with her teaching background and closeness to both Bill and me for the countless hours of reading and organizing documents.

To my niece, Katie, for taking my rough idea and using her artistic talent to create the book cover. To my granddaughter, Heather, who aided me with her legal expertise and has always been my go-to confidante.

To Bill's close friend, Tom, for his insight on scientific subjects and sharing of his strong faith in our Christian God.

A big "Thank you" to everyone who has prayed for and encouraged me through this endeavor. I hesitate to mention you by name lest I miss someone. My friends, clergy, along with many members of our blended family, my heartful appreciation for the interest and support, as well as your desire, to read this book.

Introduction

Maybe the first question to ask is, Why? Why should anyone want to get to know God? Of course, if you've already faced the question of belief in God and decided that He doesn't exist, then you probably don't care, and we can drop the whole thing. But if you do believe in God, even if it's only a sort of gut reaction, you might want to become a bit more informed on the subject. After all, there is this eternity thing that sounds kind of scary, and hopefully, there's a lot more to it than just that. Or, come to think about it, maybe the question of where and how we will spend eternity is really the ultimate question and deserves a great deal more attention than most dedicate to it.

For just a moment, let's look at eternity or infinity, which is the spatial equivalent of eternity. Either of these for most of us is a rather vague concept that just kind of floats out there in space without any real impact on us. If we've ever encountered either in any meaningful way, it's probably when we were studying mathematics, and infinity appeared in some formula that we had to memorize and maybe even use to solve a mathematical problem. But even there, it didn't impact us much outside the confines of that math course.

Jesus said that there are two things that are key—love God and love your neighbor. How do you love someone like God that you can't see or hear or sense in any way? It isn't easy. But we do have the Bible, which is the story of God's interaction with people here on earth, and there's a lot in the Bible that tells us about God. You may have to dig a bit and think about some of it a bit, and that's what I propose to do. The very first thing in the Bible talks about God creating our universe and everything in it including our earth and us. There's a good bit to learn about God from that, especially by looking at the things God made.

Next, there are all those stories about God dealing with early humankind, Adam and Eve, Noah and Abraham, etc. Again, we learn some more about God. Then there's the whole Egyptian mess and God rescuing the Israelites and enacting a covenant with them and handing down all those laws through Moses. This tells us a lot more. Finally, the Israelites enter their "promised land," and there's their struggle to become established and God's helping them and God's frustration with them and the great leaders like Joshua and David and Solomon.

This is followed by a long period when God's involvement was pretty much restricted to prophets who spoke for God, like Job, Isaiah, Jeremiah, Ezekiel, Daniel, and Malachi. Now, we come to the bonanza—Christ who is God yet is also a man who can be seen and touched and heard, the personification of God. How better to get to know God! In the New Testament, we are provided with the accounts of the apostles and early disciples, especially Paul, John, Peter, and James! They were physically here on earth with Jesus, the personification of God.

When reading the Bible, since everything recorded there is by some human (God didn't sit down and write it Himself), there's always the possible question whether that's exactly what God wanted written or whether the author might have used a bit of poetic license. However, in many places, the Bible quotes what God or Jesus said (Jesus is God too), and I believe that there's a higher degree of certainty in a quote than in narrative discussion. The speaker might not be quoted exactly word for word, but I would rely on the full meaning of the quote to be accurate. So, in our journey through the Bible, we're going to place a lot of importance in God's quotes in revealing His intention and meaning. How better to get to know God?

A Scientist's Quest for God

Before our journey begins, there are several things that you should know about me. First, I am a scientist. I have a PhD in organic chemistry from a highly regarded US university and spent several years performing chemical research and managing general scientific research programs for major US corporations. This means that my natural bent and training predispose me to approach questions of truth logically and analytically. Secondly, I have been retired for several years. Thirdly, I was brought up in and spent my adult life in what you might call a churchgoing family, but I really didn't devote much time to analyzing any potential conflict between the scientific world and my Christian commitment. Truth be told, my Christian commitment didn't impose many more constraints on my life than going to church on Sunday and occasional service on the church governing board.

All my life, I've heard the Bible read in church and myself have read it through from cover to cover at least twice. And all that time, there has been one inconsistency that has bothered me. The Bible clearly teaches that accepting Christ as your Savior imposes a never-ending struggle to get better, to emulate Christ in a life of servitude. My observation of the people around me who claimed to be Christians or even regularly attended church, including myself, was that in terms of Christian living, their commitment to Christ made very little difference in how they lived their lives. Being a Christian was more like belonging to a club; you paid your dues and attended meetings when it was convenient. And since I recognized myself in that group, it can't have bothered me too much. Not that we all were bad people, but we spent a great deal more time and effort getting ahead in life than we did worrying about the well-being of others less fortunate than ourselves.

But a few years ago, it struck me. Why do I, why do any of these self-possessed people, put up the facade of being a Christian? They must expect to get something out of it. There must be innate belief in a life after death and acceptance that the road there leads through the church. However, our happy confidence in the benefits of church membership, or even just in our baptism into the church, doesn't seem to jibe with what the Bible teaches. So I decided it was time I gave this matter some serious thought. If it were important for me to change my life, there was still time. If it wasn't, then I could quit worrying about it and enjoy life as I saw fit.

Confession

"Getting to know God" is not a topic that would interest an avowed atheist, so there's a presumption that anyone who might want to read what follows does believe that God exists or at least is curious about whether there is a God and what that God may be like. I know from personal experience that considering oneself a Christian and repeating regularly in one of the Christian creeds, "I believe in God the Father Almighty," do not necessarily make one a committed Christian. I'm going to define "committed Christian" as one in whom being a Christian makes a significant difference in how you lead your life.

Now that I've sufficiently confused the issue, let me explain what I mean in terms of my own life. I was born and raised in a churchgoing family—churchgoing, not religious! Religion was not a daily or even occasional topic in our home. I don't remember there even being a Bible in the house though my mother was an avid reader. But we did go to church. Both of my parents sang in the church choir, as did my older brother and I, from the age of six in the boys' choir and then when our voices changed in the adult choir. That also meant an hour's choir practice on Thursdays and Saturday evening from seven thirty to eight thirty. (Can you imagine getting away with that today?) But in those days, the church was as much a social as a religious focus.

There were numerous church dinners on Wednesday evenings and church bazaars, and the church sponsored the Boy Scout troop. So, for me, the church was an ever-present force in my preadult life. When I went away to college and then military service, my church attendance became sporadic, but after I married and started a family, it was back in church most every week. Ultimately, I got back into the choir and became involved on the church board and other church-related activities. The church played a significant role throughout my active adult life. All this time, I, of course, considered myself a pretty good and involved Christian.

After I retired and moved to a senior community in the southwest, I became a close friend of a fellow of Italian heritage who had received a conventional Italian Catholic upbringing but in later years had grown to question and finally completely lose his faith. He and I had several discussions on the subject, in the process of which I had to face the fact that I too had questions. How firmly did I really believe all these things that I had been taking for granted all these years? Did I really believe that I am a sinner and that I must turn my life over to God and strive to follow Jesus? Did my faith have any significant effect on how I live my life—I don't mean in the important, showy things like regularly attending church and being on various religious or charity boards, but rather, I mean in the simple and nearly invisible things like showing compassion and directly offering help to those in need? The answer that I was forced to accept told me that I'd better reexamine my faith. Did I really believe that God made the universe and that Jesus died so that my sins could be forgiven and that I must follow the kind of life that Jesus prescribed if I hope to attain eternal life?

The first and most basic question that faced me was whether the God of the Bible, the God who was in my mind, really exists. Is God provable? If I had any question about that fact, there was very little chance of my "religion" meaning anything significant other than as a show to boost my self-esteem. So I started to dig into what's really known about the origin of the universe.

Having been educated and worked as a scientist, I approach questions like this first by looking for proven facts before drawing any conclusions. What I found was that there is good, sound scientific evidence that our universe did have a finite starting point, both in time and in space. There's even a well-accepted explanation as to how this happened, called the big bang theory. We'll talk more about that in the chapter "God the Creator." However, the conclusion that I must draw is that since this event occurred, it had to have a cause, and that cause had to predate the formation of the universe and must be outside the universe. That is basic and uncontestable logic. It also seems, however, from the enormous dimensions of this process, and from its exquisite complexity, whatever force or entity caused it to come about must have possessed unbelievable intellect and power to be able to plan and execute it.

So as far as I am concerned, we have a first fact—the universe and everything in it, including us, was created! I totally reject the suggestion that our universe has just always been here or, even what is more unacceptable, that the universe just happened to form in response to natural laws. What natural laws? Before our natural universe existed, there were no natural laws. The natural laws exist only because of the existence and composition of the natural world, our physical universe.

So the universe must have been created, but who or what was responsible for that creation is another question, a question of just as great significance for our religious beliefs as the first one. Unfortunately, my scientific approach provides no further answers. We cannot prove that God exists, nor can we prove that God was the creator of our universe! That belief we must take on faith. Of course, my belief framework was well in place. I had been "in church" all my life. All it really took was a good nudge—really, maybe, a jolt. For me, the thoughtfully reached realization that our world had, in fact, been created was what was needed to energize my faith. I won't say that I was reborn. It was more that I now had confidence that all this dogma that I had been carrying has real and true meaning and that I had better get about doing instead of mostly just saying. Of course, I can't deny the possibility, at least in part, that my commitment to God and all that that entails could be influenced by my need for assurance of some personal existence after death and for a purpose to life other than just to get all that I can get. Nor have I magically, overnight, become a saint. Far from it. I am still, and always will be, a sinner. That's true of us all, but I have found that I'm more aware of that fact and actively try to do something about it. Salvation is not a fait accompli, but a lifetime process. Hopefully, I'm making progress, and a large part of that is getting to know God more fully.

The Bible Interpretation

Since we've decided to use the Bible as our source of information in "getting to know God," it would be well first to
say a few things about what information the Bible contains and how to deal with the things that are said there.
The Bible is a chronology of the interaction of God with
humankind from the creation of the physical or material
world as we know it until sometime in the first or early
second century AD. It tells of God as the planner and
creator of our world. It tells of His interaction with early
humankind, of His selection of a specific family or people
on which to focus His attention. Finally, it tells of God's
sending a messiah, His Son Jesus, to complete His active,
visible interaction with humankind.

Clearly, humans wrote the Bible, and since it was first
written, a great deal has been learned by humans about
our universe, the earth, and life on this earth. Thus, much
language that is used in the Bible describes these subjects
in terms that could be understood by early humankind,
and it is not surprising that much of this language conflicts
with what has since been learned. Even so, most Christian
authorities believe that the content of the Bible is completely God inspired. It is almost universally accepted
that the first five books of the Bible (Genesis, Exodus,
Leviticus, Numbers, and Deuteronomy) were written by

Moses. These too are the foundation of the Jewish sacred writings and are known as the Torah. Following the writings of Moses, the authorship of the remainder of the Old Testament is less clear. Most authorities agree that when we reach the long list of prophets from Isaiah to Malachi, the named person was at least a major contributor. The New Testament books are credited to men who lived closely with Jesus during his ministry and while He was on earth following His resurrection. The two notable exceptions to this are Paul and Luke—Paul, who was selected by Jesus following His ascension to carry the "good news" to the Gentiles, and Luke, who was a close associate of Paul. The entire New Testament was written in the first or very early second century AD.

Why do I tell you all of this? I do it to emphasize that in many cases authorship is uncertain or unknown, and in no case do we possess the original manuscript or clay tablet on which they were written. In no way, however, does this mean that these are not the Word of God or that what is said there does not concur with God's intent. However, the languages in which the earliest extant documents were written are either Hebrew, Greek, or Aramaic; and even those earliest sources are obviously the result of sequences of copying and probably, before that, the spoken word. Add to that, the Bibles that we read today are the result of translations from those original languages. Even though these translations are the result of intensive scholarly study and research, they are translations! This means that a precise word-for-word translation in many cases is not possible, and the best that scholarly translation can provide is to transfer the intended meaning of a given passage.

I dwell on this point for one reason. There are those who insist, dogmatically insist, that every word in the Bible is to be taken as true, literal, and inviolable. Add to that the fact that when these writings were first composed, human knowledge about our physical world was primitive, and the written word had to be such as would be understood at that time. This can lead to some surprising, even ridiculous, interpretations. With my scientific background, I find some of these completely unacceptable. On the other hand, I accept that God is not bound by the laws of our physical world. I don't reject miracles, though I find walking on water or turning water into wine tough to handle. But it's not these, or curing physical defects or diseases, that I have trouble with. After all, this is God who's involved, and if He can create our universe, what's to say He can't do these things as well. Where I do get hung up is insisting that the universe was created in six actual days or that creation started just six thousand years ago or that after humankind and all other animal life were already established on earth, everything was covered by a layer of water sufficient to exterminate all existing life except for those people and animals floating in a boat. None of these make any scientific or common sense, and there are very reasonable and scientifically sound alternatives, so why go so far out of line desperately to try to prove your point, especially when your point isn't really that critical? After all, does exactly how the earth was created or whether there was a life-destroying flood really make any difference in whether we get the true message intended by God? Isn't it much more likely that God accepted language that conveyed His essential meaning and would be understood by those early readers?

Now if I were an eminent theologian, I might expect that you could pay some heed to this ranting, but since I'm just an old guy who puttered around with science and business, what do I know about theology? I too was kind of concerned about whether my opinions would be heeded, so I went digging on the Internet and found that some others who had deeper religious roots than I had similar concerns. How about Origen of Alexandria, a preeminent Christian scholar, theologian, and one of the most distinguished writers of the early church, who, according to Wikipedia, wrote in the early third century (that's in the AD 200s) in his *De Principiis IV* when speaking of the Genesis creation story,

> For who that has understanding will suppose that the first, and second, and third day, and the evening and the morning, existed without a sun, and moon, and stars? And that the first day was, as it were, also without a sky? And who is so foolish as to suppose that God, after the manner of a husbandman, planted a paradise in Eden, towards the east, and placed in it a tree of life, visible and palpable, so that one tasting of the fruit by the bodily teeth obtained life? And again, that one was a partaker of good and evil by masticating what was taken from the tree? And if God is said to walk in the paradise in the evening, and Adam to hide himself under a tree, I do not suppose that anyone doubts that these things figuratively indicate cer-

tain mysteries, the history having taken place in appearance, and not literally.

Also, according to Wikipedia,

St. Augustine, one of the most influential theologians of the Catholic Church, suggested that the Biblical text should not be interpreted literally if it contradicts what we know from science and our God-given reason. From an important passage on his '*The Literal Interpretation of Genesis*' (early fifth century, AD), St. Augustine wrote:

It not infrequently happens that something about the earth, about the sky, about other elements of this world, about the motion and rotation or even the magnitude and distances of the stars, about definite eclipses of the sun and moon, about the passage of years and seasons, about the nature of animals, of fruits, of stones, and of other such things, may be known with the greatest certainty by reasoning or by experience, even by one who is not a Christian. It is too disgraceful and ruinous, though, and greatly to be avoided, that he [the non-Christian] should hear a Christian speaking so idiotically on these matters, and as if in accord with Christian writings, that he might say that he could scarcely keep from laughing when he saw how totally in error they are.

In view of this and in keeping it in mind constantly while dealing with the book of Genesis, I have, insofar as I was able, explained in detail and set forth for consideration the meanings of obscure passages, taking care not to affirm rashly someone meaning to the prejudice of another and perhaps better explanation.

And much more recently but no less authoritatively, in 1981, when writing to the Pontifical Academy of Sciences, Pope John Paul II stated,

Cosmogony and cosmology have always aroused great interest among peoples and religions. The Bible itself speaks to us of the origin of the universe and its make-up, not in order to provide us with a scientific treatise, but in order to state the correct relationships of man with God and with the universe. Sacred Scripture wishes simply to declare that God created the world, and in order to teach this truth it expresses itself in the terms of the cosmology in use at the time of the writer. The Sacred Book likewise wishes to tell men that the world was not created as the seat of the gods, as was taught by other cosmogonies and cosmologies, but was rather created for the service of man and the glory of God. Any other teaching about the origin and make-up of the universe is alien to the intentions of the Bible, which does not wish to teach how heaven was made but how one goes to heaven. ("Pope John Paul II on Creationism" National Center for Science Education, https://ncse.ngo/pope-john-paul-ii-creationism)

So I am not alone in suggesting that some of the biblical teachings are stated allegorically, in picturesque language. When you read the Bible, then you should look first and foremost for the meaning and significance of what God is saying in that passage. What is God's message? If something said there contradicts common sense or current scientific knowledge, set it aside until you feel that you understand the truth that God is teaching and then assess whether the precise content of the passage in question is critical to an understanding of that truth. For example, in the first two chapters of Genesis, the important truth that God is teaching is that He created our universe, including the earth and life on earth. That tells us emphatically that God is responsible for everything that we are or have and for that deserves our continual thanks and praise. It also must signify something of the love that He feels for us and that we should return to Him. In order to appreciate the magnitude of that gift, is it important whether that creation took place in six days or billions of years or are any of the other details that are in conflict important to that appreciation? I'll treat each of these contradictions as it arises in our journey through the Bible, but in no instance are the questioned details the truth that is being taught.

When I am faced with a question about what God would say about this or that subject, I turn first to the gospels and, if I don't find the answer there, next to the epistles of Paul and the other disciples. Why do I do this? Why do I almost totally ignore the Old Testament as a source of guidance and direction in my life? God can't have intended that. Jesus taught and relied on the Old Testament completely as the source for teaching "the way" during His ministry here on earth. No, that's not quite right. Jesus amplified and explained the teachings of the Old Testament as the "good news" of the new covenant. After all, during Jesus's time on earth the New Testament didn't exist. Jesus hadn't "written" it yet.

Still, the Old Testament amounts to nearly three-quarters of our Holy Scripture, so God must have had some reason for giving it such a powerful significance in the lives and history of His "chosen people." Jesus Himself said, "Do not think that I have come to abolish the law or the prophets; I have come not to abolish but to fulfill" (Matthew 5:17). So what is the significance of the Old Testament? First, it presents that vital declaration of the creation by God. All the rest of the Old Testament and New Testament would hold no meaning if it weren't for that. The remainder of the Old Testament tells of God's open interaction with humankind, first with the prehistoric people Adam and Eve and Noah and then of His selection of a specific family as His chosen people through Abraham and finally on and on dealing with them as reluctant and recalcitrant failures in His hope of getting them to live a "good life" in accordance with His set of rules. It seems that God was destined to disappointment and frustration in His high hopes for humankind's loving relationship with Him. People continued to be people, doing what people inherently do because of their nature, looking out for number one. Even in the face of God's persistent admonishments and punishments, humankind's powerful self-interests prevailed.

At this point, it would be easy to look at God as dumb. After a dozen or so tries, you'd think God would get the picture. These people that God created just aren't interested, or capable, of following a bunch of laws that require them to deny themselves pleasure or satisfaction at times. You'd think God would catch on, at least if God's as smart as we're told. And that's the point. To assume that God learned or changed his mind is denying what God is. God is omniscient, omnipotent, and eternal. That's what God is. God knows everything, everything that's happening now, everything that will happen, and everything that's happened in the past. So, by His very nature, God knows how the Israelites are going to react. The whole point of God's interaction with them over centuries is not to teach God, but to teach the Israelites, and us, that by ourselves we're hopelessly sinful and that without God's help there's no way we can be close to God and be the kind of people that God wants us to be. It's all preparation for the coming of the Messiah, for the coming of Jesus. To justify and understand God's sacrifice in sending Christ to die for our sins, we must understand that we are incapable of turning to God through a set of rules and laws alone. The laws remain as measures of our goodness, but we, by our very nature, are going to disobey no matter how hard we may think we try.

This might be a good time to delve more into the nature of God. Many of the problems that we experience in understanding the Bible or some of the actions of God arise from our instinctively applying human or natural world limitations or measurements to things of God. First and foremost, God is not of this world (John 8:23). God created this world, so obviously God is outside the thing that He made. Obviously, then too God is not physical. God does not have substance, height and breadth, and depth and mass as do all things of the physical world. God is spirit (John 4:24) and resides in the spirit world. What that means is outside the scope of our understanding. Human knowledge is based on and limited to human experience—only what we can see, hear, or feel—and that's limited to things of the physical world. So we cannot see God, we cannot hear God, we cannot physically feel God, and we cannot even prove, scientifically, the existence of God.

So we get into problems in our perception of and reaction to God. We call God "He." We assign a gender. Why? Well, God is an authority figure, and authority figures—certainly in the times when the Bible was written—were male. Not only is God male, but also because we associate wisdom with age, He is an old male with long white hair and beard. Why, in the spirit world, would there be any reason for gender as we know it? Gender only exists in the physical world to facilitate reproduction. As far as we know, that's not an aspect of the spirit world, so we should eliminate it from our thinking of God.

Throughout the following pages, I will try not to use pronouns to reference God. It may at times get a bit repetitive, God this and God that, but it will avoid the gender problem. So, for now, we must force ourselves to back off from assigning physical attributes and physical restrictions to God and focus on those things about God that we know from the Bible's teachings. First, there's the language problem. Every time I write anything about God, almost immediately I run into the problem of what to do about pronouns—he, his, and him. I suppose I could use it to refer to God, but that would too harshly demean its majesty. Even with he, him and his, we traditionally capitalize them. The English language needs a genderless, timeless name for God. The Jews and Muslims have tried with Yahweh or Jehovah and Allah, but none of those eliminate the pronoun problem, unless you simply refrain from using pronouns at all. If we do that, the word God works. It just gets a whit cumbersome after the fifteenth repetition. Unless I want to bore deeply into lexicography, for which I'm neither qualified nor inclined, I'm afraid I'm going to have to use God without pronouns.

We put God in a place. Everybody must be someplace, so we call the place where God is heaven, and we put it "up there, above" and give heaven physical attributes like golden gates and jewel-encrusted streets and buildings. We forget that there was nothing physical before God created our physical universe, but God and the place where God lives obviously predate all this and can't be a part of it. God—and therefore the place where God lives—is eternal. God cannot be contained within our physical world. God may be present in it but reside outside in the spirit world.

But since God made the universe, the universe must be contained in the spirit world, but not in a physical sense available to it. Not until our individual deaths release us from the restrictions and limitations of this physical world will we be free to join God in the spirit world, and when that happens, for the first time we will know what God and the spirit world are really like.

Time—what about time and God? In our physical world, time has the vital importance of a primary dimension along with length, width, and height. Time and length or distance are so intimately intertwined that we even measure time in terms of a physical dimension. How long is a day, week, month, year? The amazing *distance* in astronomy, such as how long a light year is that we can't even force our minds to be comfortable with. Then we have *time* interrelations such as *soon, lately,* and *next.* There are also *place* interrelations such as *here, there, outside, inside,* etc. Our language is so entangled with measurements of all kinds. But what about time and place in the spirit world, in heaven? In an infinite and eternal world, time and place don't exist, at least as we know them. The only time that counts is now, and the only place, here. So, for God, our lifetime here on earth is no longer than a second and no shorter than an eon. The second coming is, was, and will be. I'm not suggesting that God is unmindful of our basic dependence on time and space relationships, but that when we begin to impose those same attributes on God, we are imposing limitations and misrepresentations on God's nature and actions.

The very first thing the Bible tells us about God is of His (yikes, I just did it) prodigious intellect and unbelievable power as Creator of this immense and majestic universe of which our planet earth and our very selves are, to us, a vital part. Did God do all of this to provide us a place to live? Our egos would like to think this, but fortunately we'll never on this earth find out. We are told that we are created in the very image of God. Since we have no idea what God looks like, we immediately transpose the intended meaning of that revelation and create God in our image. We've done it again. Perhaps it doesn't mean "physical image." In fact, with God, it can't mean physical. Could it mean the same intellectual, emotional, and moral image? The same image, but much less focused and much fuzzier, the image of God as an aspiration! That truly is where Jesus is directing us when He says, "And follow me." The next thing we learn is that God is a social being. God is pleased with creation and enjoys being in it and sharing it with the people created. I have a bit of a problem with God walking through the garden of Eden with Adam and Eve, but I have a bigger problem with God being fooled into thinking that these created beings would be compliant and obey God's every wish, including not eating the fruit of the tree. God knew the outcome in advance, as God always knows the future. In a sense, we are as God created us, rebellious, inquisitive, and self-serving. The toughest lesson that we learn, and many of us never do, is that the truest happiness and the greatest spiritual achievement come through service to others. It's not foreign to our nature, if only we can sublimate our egos and self-interest.

Throughout the Old Testament, repeatedly we see evidence of God being gracious and loving. Often that love is of the kind called tough love. Repeatedly the Israelites have rebelled against God's laws and have had to be corrected and punished. Often the punishment seems unduly harsh. We have become familiar with tough love often because of substance abuse programs like AA, so a tough love response from God should not surprise us since our rebellion is of the nature of an addiction, an incurable addiction. Sometimes in the Old Testament, we must dig a bit to find God's love and grace, but it's always there. In the New Testament, it hits us in the face! Jesus's ministry here on earth is a gospel of love. It is Jesus who describes God as love. It is Jesus who defines our total purpose as loving God and loving our neighbors. If we are to become godlike, we must emulate God in loving totally. Simple, but for us, impossible. Not for God, however. God submitted to the agony of a horrible death so that we, who believe, might have our sins forgiven and be saved. That's love! In that last sentence, we just tripped over another aspect of the nature of God, the triune God. Some might question, "Who died on the cross? Jesus, the Son of God, not God the Father!" Do you think that God's pain and passion were diminished because it was the Son and not the Father who experienced it—a difficult aspect of God's nature?

God's forgiveness astonishes us throughout the Bible. Again and again in the Old Testament, God forgives the Israelites their transgressions, at times it seems ad nauseam. A succinct accounting of the roller-coaster ride of the Israelites in their relationship with God is given in Nehemiah 9:6–31. In every instance, after God showered blessings and miracles on them, the Israelites responded with disobedience and sacrilege, and God forgave them. Is not that the history of a remorselessly forgiving God? Jesus, on the other hand, demonstrated forgiveness in a much more personal way—His forgiving of the woman caught in adultery, those He healed, the blind, the lame, the lepers, and, the most personal of all forgiveness's, those who so cruelly killed Him and for us the most essential forgiveness of our sins, which, otherwise, would have separated us from God throughout eternity. Compassion is different from love, in that it needs first sin or disaster to bring it into being. It's something that is felt in the face of the misfortune of others. It is intimately related to love and a precursor of forgiveness. It is of the essence of "love your neighbor." It, also, is difficult to generate compassion if the misfortune has befallen one who is unlovable or, even worse, may have performed some act perceived as hostile against us. God, clearly, is compassionate. Is God judgmental? There is enough talk in the Bible about the day of judgment to render that question moot. Jesus even tells us that judgment is God's prerogative alone. However, I feel certain that whatever action results from God's judgment will be directed toward refreshing our relationship with God rather than punishment for our past sins. If I didn't hold this hope, what a dismal promise eternity would offer. Which of us would have the temerity to look forward to streets of gold and jewel-encrusted thrones based on our performance in this life? We can only rely on God's compassion.

We have talked briefly about God's nature, that God is immensely creative; that God is social and wants to be near us and loved by us and communicate with us; that God is gracious, loving, compassionate, and forgiving; and that judgment belongs to God alone with the sole purpose of redirecting and improving our lives and our relationship with God and our fellow human beings. If we are serious about getting to know God better, it's important that we dwell on these attributes of God in more detail. But how do you get to know or get close to someone whom you cannot see, hear, touch, or feel in any tangible way? It seems like a hopeless undertaking. I don't have a detailed, well-documented plan for this critical task. Getting to know God is a journey that I too am on, and at times I feel that I've lost my way. I suspect that you've already anticipated what I'm going to suggest, the Bible and prayer. But is there anything else? The Bible contains everything that we know about God and God's expectations for us. I challenge anyone to pick up and read the Bible regularly and not be surprised by the things you discover about God. And since God is a social being, talking to and praying are the best and only way we have of communicating with God. We have been assured that God hears our prayers and answers them. If we take the initiative in communicating with God, we've got to trust that God will somehow respond in a way that we can understand.

Our search for God is going to take us through the Bible, both Old Testament and New Testament, and our approach largely will involve looking for those places when God talked to humans. I am amazed at how many times God is quoted in the Old Testament. In the gospels of the New Testament, a large part of the message is Jesus (God) talking to the apostles or others, but I didn't remember how many times God spoke to humans in the Old Testament. In the book of Genesis, God talked to almost all the major characters—Adam, Eve, Cain, Noah, Abram frequently, Sarai, Abimelech, Lot, Isaac, Rebecca, and

Jacob. In Exodus 3, through the burning bush, God spoke to Moses and directed him to return to Egypt and lead the Israelites to freedom. God continued to direct Moses until they had fled and crossed the Red Sea and entered Sinai. In Exodus 20, God hands down the Ten Commandments; and throughout the remainder of Exodus, Leviticus, and Numbers, paragraph after paragraph begins with the words, "The Lord spoke to Moses" or Aaron or Moses and Aaron, where God defines in detail how the Israelites are to conduct their worship and their daily lives (the Law of Moses).

The entire religious experience might be summed up as "getting to know God." That presupposes, of course, that first you believe there is a god. Once we've made that leap of faith, that decision or maybe just hope, that says there must be a force, an intelligence, a being that is responsible for the planning, the design, and the creation of this amazing universe of which we are a part, the rest of the journey through life is getting to know more and more about that being.

Every civilization, every society, every people, clan, or tribe throughout history has created its own god or gods to account for and explain the frightening and awesome experiences of life. So we have the sun god, the god of thunder, of the sea, of lightning, and so on. As knowledge grew and society became more sophisticated, religion too became less a matter of fear and focused more on human attributes and emotions like love and beauty, wisdom, evil, and war. The ancient Greeks even created Zeus, the chief god, the father of the gods to rule over the rest.

It was the Israelites who first proclaimed a single god, or rather, as our historical experience and record teaches,

God selected the Israelites through whom He would make Himself and His interactions with them known to our world. The record of those interactions is detailed in the Old Testament and New Testament of the Bible. The Old Testament tells of human failure and God's frustration, as humankind, starting with Adam and Eve, choose to satisfy self rather than to follow God's rules of behavior. There are some who will insist that it took God an unbelievably long time to realize that humans are so self-oriented that they will not or cannot adhere to a set of rules of behavior. I contend that such cannot be, because such a position ignores a fundamental characteristic of God. God is all-powerful and all-knowing; thus, God cannot be surprised by the future. God knew from the beginning. God planned the creation and gave humankind the freedom to choose between right and wrong. God knew that it would require an extended history of humankind's unwillingness, actual inability, to obey before we would accept that fact. Even they, though chosen by God to be God's special people, demonstrated a repeated, frustrating human reluctance to accept a single, sovereign god and obey his laws and rules of conduct, thus the endless stories recounted throughout the Old Testament of God's repeated attempts and repeated failures to establish an ongoing and workable relationship with the descendants of Abraham.

The Bible

When seeking answers to questions of proper Christian conduct or behavior, the most fundamental, yes, and trust-worthy source of answers has to be the Bible. This is God's Word from which all legitimate religious beliefs and prac-tices derive. True, there are differences of interpretation among the various Christian denominations, some truly significant while others more trivial or procedural. There is general acceptance, however, that the words written down in the Bible are God-inspired. The earliest available man-uscripts were in Aramaic, Hebrew, and Greek; but to my knowledge, none of the original writings survived into his-torical times. Our access today to the original words must come through copies and translations, and we must trust that these were made with loving care and devotion to the original thought and intent.

The Bible is more or less a historical record of God's interaction with humankind, starting with God's decision to create this material world, our universe and all that is in it, including us. One thing we must keep always close to the surface when we speak of God, or try to understand or visualize God, is that God is not of this material (physical) world in which we live and whose dimensions and limita-tions very much define our thinking and language.

God is spirit, and the Bible tells us that "He is not of this world." God is of the spirit world, whatever and wherever that is! God is not a white-haired old man in a flowing white robe sitting on a cloud. God is probably not a man at all, nor a woman. Gender clearly is related to our world and probably doesn't exist in the spirit world since it would serve to purpose, but of course, we don't know.

However, in these times, gender is one place where we get into trouble in the Bible. Equality of the sexes is a very real, valid, and often vocal subject today; but thirty-five hundred years ago, when Moses wrote the first five books of the Old Testament, a woman's place was in the home, and man was the authority figure. So Moses began the practice of referring to God as "He," and this practice continues throughout the remainder of the books of the Bible. The same also becomes a problem in referring to "man" or "mankind" in the generic sense. We've been forced to rewrite a lot of our hymns changing such words to "humans" or "people" or "humankind" and often resulting in acceptable, but awkward, gender-neutral wording.

One other matter concerning the Bible that needs to deal with before I get into discussions of commands and other statements and their meanings is the question of "inerrancy." There are Christians who believe that every single word in the Bible is literally and unequivocally true, not only the thought conveyed but also the individual words. Aside from some of the ridiculous conflicts with scientific knowledge that this causes, I've always wondered how such a position handles the fact that every Bible today results from a translation, and in many instances, different translation uses slightly different words and phrasing, even meanings for a given passage. That's the first general problem that I have with inerrancy. The second is that some of the language and even entire events described in the Bible are so grossly in conflict with not only scientific knowledge but also plain common sense and reason. How, for example, can you describe the first two phases of the process of creation as having occurred in single days when the sun is created until the third day? After all, the "day" is the length of time it takes for any individual point on the earth to compete a single rotation relative to the sun. That being true, days as we know them couldn't have passed before the sun existed. Another problem—Noah and the flood. Two of every animal, male and female, supposedly from all over the earth, since the flood was going to destroy all existing flesh. Also, where did all the water come from? Unanswerable questions, unless one attributes the entire biblical event to one of God's colossal miracles.

Miracles—I must be perfectly clear from the outset that I do not discount the possibility or truth of miracles. I *believe* that God created the universe we live in; whether it happened in six days or more than thirteen billion years does not diminish the magnitude or miraculous nature of that event. I *believe* that Christ walked on water and performed healing miracles. I *believe* that Christ brought people back to life, not from apparent but actual death. Why is this hard for some to believe, for a God who could perform the *miracle* of creation? Here again, we tend to place human and physical world limitations on God, who is not so limited, since He made the whole mess in the first place. No, *miracles* have and still do occur, but they happen when and where God selects, not us.

What, then, do I feel about the message of the Bible? First, I believe that numerous events and situations in the Bible, especially in the Old Testament, are allegorical rather than factual. The whole matter of the creation of the universe, the earth and us, was so far beyond the understanding of primitive people that God had to provide descriptions that would have meaning for them. For that matter, we've made tremendous progress in the understanding of the physical world, but still the best we can do with creation is an unproven theory. But that does not diminish the wonder and magnitude of the event; rather to me, it makes it even more wondrous. Another area where I have a problem with taking the Bible message as being inerrant is where God is surprised by events and their consequences. This is a God who is all-knowing and omniscient, who obviously knows the future, and who repeatedly has accurately prophesied it. Why then does it come as a surprise to God that we humans are self-serving or, even at times, cruel? Can you believe that God didn't know that Adam and Eve would eat of the apple when cautioned not to (if Adam and Eve and the garden of Eden aren't also allegorical)? Did not know that humankind would turn out to be corrupt and need cleansing (again, allegorical)? Time as we know it is a dimension of a limited, physical world. But God is not of this world. It is speculated that for God, the only time is now—whichever "now" God elects to consider at the moment—yesterday, a hundred years ago, tomorrow, or a billion years ago. It's pretty much all the same when compared to eternity. God prophesied the coming of Christ hundreds of years in advance. In Revelation, God has prophesied the end of our world or universe. So how can such a God be surprised by what happens here on earth? No, I can only surmise that all these accounts of the corruption of humankind and the repeated failures of the Israelites to be true to God are presented as compelling evidence to us of our inherent inability to obey God's rules for our behavior. God made us for what we are; how could God be surprised at how we turned out?

In the book of Exodus, through the Ten Commandments and the explanation and amplification provided in the remainder of that book, God has made it clear to the Israelites what is expected of them to live an acceptable life in God's eye. In Leviticus, God has given detailed instructions on what offerings the Israelites must sacrifice for the atonement of specific unintentional sins. God shows very clearly that sacrifice is required and expected for them to receive forgiveness even if the sin was not premeditated. However, over the years, over the centuries, again and again, the Israelites continued to fall away, as a nation and as individuals, from God's design and desires.

And, of course, that's where Jesus enters the picture. He came from God, as God, in human form, to show us in plainly understandable human actions and words what God wants and expects of us in order to be with God throughout eternity, knowing full well that we are inherently incapable of fulfilling those demands. There would always be a negative balance on our behavior ledger for which we owe sacrificial offerings, but I can only assume that God decided that it now was time to end the slaughtering of animals to atone for our sins. In its place, God made the ultimate sacrifice, once and all time, by offering Jesus Christ, God's only Son, to be the only necessary atonement for our sins, past, present, and future. All that is needed is for us to believe this, that Jesus in the Son of God, that He died for our sins but was raised from the dead and returned to God His Father, and that we should follow the teachings and example of Jesus. And therein lies the rub! What exactly does it mean to "follow"? My feeling is that the purpose of what I am doing here is to examine the things Jesus said and did, trying to understand how they relate to questions of behavior that arise in our daily lives to specific issues we face today. I don't pretend to have any special or unique insight that has been denied to theologians over the centuries. Let's take a closer look at some of the books in the Bible that will help unearth some answers for us.

God the Creator

Before we delve too deeply into the book of Genesis, we should develop a position on how to interpret much of the language found there. There are those who insist that every word, every statement, in the Bible is literally true, an absolute and unquestionable fact. The problem that I have is that, as I progress through the early books of the Bible, I soon begin to stumble over some of the things described—some things claimed or described there simply do not seem reasonable or possible, some even ridiculous in the face of present-day knowledge. Starting at the very beginning of Genesis, the specifics of the creation story are often inconsistent or even in opposition to one another. The sun isn't created until the fourth day, but the sun is a necessary ingredient to allow the observation and measurement of the passage of a day's time. In the first creation account, the animals are created before man. In the second creation account, they are created after. In the first account, man and woman are created on the same day. In the second account, woman is created from one of the ribs of the man. These are irreconcilable problems if we insist on inerrancy. Go further, the closest star to earth other than the sun is 4.2 light-years away (we know this from scientific measurement), which means that if that star were created today, it wouldn't even be seen for over four years. The rest of the stars wouldn't appear until hundreds, thousands, millions, or even billions of years later, not on a single day as the Bible says.

This problem of reasonable concurrence between biblical accounts and current knowledge is one that has been dealt with since the early years of the Christian church.

For these reasons, my attitude when dealing with questionable scientific foundation is let science—which has both the tools and the authority to deal with what, when, and how of our universe—do so and let religion confine itself to our relationship with God and each other. Thus, where the Bible states that the world was made in six days or any other biblical assertions that contradict established fact or sound ridiculous in light of present knowledge, let these statements be considered as figurative or allegorical language and be interpreted in that light. Since the Bible contains everything that is necessary for my salvation, I can't see that my salvation is going to depend in any way upon whether I believe that the universe was formed in six days or billions of years.

Open your Bible to the very first page, Genesis 1:1, and what do you see? "In the beginning God created the heavens and the earth." That's where it all begins! That fact that God created all the material world has to be primal in our belief and in our understanding of God. First, if we don't believe this, none of the rest makes any sense. In both the Apostles' Creed and Nicene Creed, which describe the essential features of our Christian belief, we begin with a statement that God is "Creator" or "Maker of heaven and earth." True, but do we really give much thought to the significance of that statement? Isn't it more likely that we have just sort of absorbed that belief along with the remainder of our faith as we have grown, without giving a lot of thoughtful attention to its critical importance? The more value we place on our personal existence and material possessions, the more highly must we revere and praise the One who provided these. Unless that foundation is firm and solid, the rest of the structure of our faith is flimsy and vulnerable.

Where does it all start? God created. Before that, there was nothing to be concerned about and no one to be concerned. How much do we really know about the creation of our universe? Did it just happen, or has it always been here? Do the findings of our natural science explain where it all came from? I found that, like most fields of science, astronomy and cosmology have taken amazing strides in the past fifty years or so. We've learned a great deal about our universe and how it was formed. We know that the universe is expanding at a measurable rate and in a predictable fashion. With that knowledge and using calculations based on Einstein's general relativity theory, physicists and cosmologists have extrapolated the expansion of the universe backward in time to a single starting point at a finite time in the past, 13.75 billion years ago. This point was infinitely small but contained all of the mass that makes up the universe compressed in space at infinite pressure—and is called a "singularity"—and was the point of creation for our universe, which has been expanding and forming ever since. This is a theory, not a proven fact, and is called the big bang theory. The proposal of this theory has generated a good bit of discussion and debate among experts in the relevant fields of science, but today it stands as the best-accepted explanation for the creation of our universe. Experiments run on large particle accelerators have tended to support the big bang theory, but we're still a long way from proving it scientifically.

Of course, there are other theories as to how the universe was formed, and even if the big bang does explain how the universe was formed, "you certainly can't prove that a god did it!" I'll have to agree, and I know that some who hold these feelings are eminent scientists, as are some who hold God as the Creator. But there's one thing I do know from all this—something had to be responsible for the creation of our universe, because good scientific reason points to the fact that it did start to form at a time and in a place. It hasn't just always been here; and whatever caused it to be formed, no matter what or who it was, had to predate and exist outside of our universe, outside of the material world as we know it, outside of what was formed. And you don't have to look too deeply into the incredibly complex and beautifully intricate world of which we are a part to realize that the planning and execution of such an amazing process or series of processes didn't just happen and that it demanded an intellect and power far in excess of anything that we could even imagine. To me, it isn't even important that the big bang theory be scientifically proven to be true. If science finds some more readily accepted theory, whatever replaces the big bang has also to have a cause, to which all of the above applies. Whatever caused the creation of our universe cannot be of our universe, but must be outside and predate our universe.

Even though I have reached the firm belief that our universe was created and thus had to have a creator, I am forced to abandon the scientific method in proving that this creator was the Christian God, or any other god. Our science exists to understand and explain our natural world. It is axiomatic then that it cannot be expected to explain what a part of that world is not, and by the most fundamental law of reason, the cause cannot be a part of the result. So why should I be surprised that I cannot explain the existence or nature of the creator of our "natural world" by using our natural science?

Where does this leave us? We cannot prove the existence of God. We could just throw up our hands and accept that all of this is unknowable and live our lives as best suits us. This life here on earth is all there is, so just enjoy it as best you can and forget all this eternity stuff. This is what the atheist does, and atheists don't necessarily lead more selfish or dishonest lives that do a lot of churchgoers. But for atheists, death is the end! I can't dismiss the eternity issue so cavalierly. If all this God stuff is true, and if how we live our lives here on earth does have a determining impact on how we are going to spend eternity, then that question should assume an overwhelming importance!

The only "evidence" we have of the existence of God is the written accounts in the Bible of God's interaction with us and our natural world. True, humans have written all of these, and it is only by subsequent assertion that God's authorship or inspiration has been established. More recently, much on this subject has also been written that attempts to show the concurrence between biblical prophecies and recorded historic events or biblical statements and recent archeological or scientific findings; but much of what has been written is by evangelical zealots who have a primary need for the "truth found" to justify their religious message and existence and who, in most of these "studies," have interpreted quite liberally rather picturesque or poetic Bible language.

Perhaps the most compelling evidence for the "truth" of the Bible could be the centuries of sacrificial service, often service to the point of martyrdom, which has been rendered in support of the Bible's teachings. Such a magnificent response cannot be regarded lightly. Theirs was a life dominated by faith. They knew that it was only through faith that their lives could be fulfilled, and thus, they acted on their faith. How can we ignore or deny the truth of their actions? Why should it seem strange for us material-dominated humans to rely on faith in our acceptance of a spirit God?

We are left with only faith to confirm our acceptance of God's existence and nature. That being the case, then isn't it reasonable when dealing with an "unknowable being" such as God to first look at the things that we can see, feel, hear, touch, and smell that God has made? We accept that God made our world and the entire universe, so God's indelible imprint must be on all of it. And when we savor these things, we rapidly develop a feeling for the grandeur and mystery of God's nature. (One of my first acts is going to be to recapture that powerful word of the English language that this current generation has stolen from us, awesome.) We meet these awesome creations of God routinely in our lives, usually taking them for granted and not reflectively as they deserve. A rosebud, a cloudless night sky, a newborn baby, a desert sunset, a tranquil rural valley, a raging surf, an armadillo, a warbler's song—these and on and on and on tell us a great deal about this awesome God who created them all and whom we thus worship.

That last sentence contains the essence of our faith and one of the most critical aspects of our relationship with God. Everything—everything that we know, everything that we need and depend upon, everything that we desire and love—was created and given to us by God! That includes us, our very selves. Is there, then, any other way in which we could regard God but with wonder, all-encompassing thankfulness, and praise? And that too often is missing from our practice of our faith in our daily lives. Aren't we frequently too eager to claim personal credit for the good and happy things that happen in our lives and to blame God for those that are bad or unfortunate? Too often we say, "How could You let this happen?" but not "thank You" for this or that. So the very first knowledge that should be imprinted in the forefront of our hearts is that everything, all of it, comes from God, and we should praise and worship God for it!

Before we leave the creation story, there's one more aspect of God's account of the process that is worth mentioning. I bring this up only because two contentious arguments that have raged between Christian groups, one for many years and the other much more recently, deal with different interpretations of that story. The first deals with the question of whether creation took place in six twenty-four-hour days as the Bible seems to state or in a number of billions of years as current scientific knowledge suggests. My answer to that is, What possible difference does it make so far as our faith is concerned? The overwhelming impact is that God did it, not how or how long it took. In God's infinite time frame, any two measurable periods of time are essentially the same. Measurement implies a starting and an ending point. When, as in eternity, there is no beginning or end to time, there also is no beginning or end to an individual period of time. So a twenty-four-hour day or an eon is as much as the same. Being a scientist, I steer clearly to science for the answer, even realizing that science may still be a long way from the full explanation. Should you cling steadfast to the biblical six days (I'm forced to ask how it could be strictly so when three of those creation days are reported to have come and gone without even the existence of the sun)? The sun and moon weren't created until the fourth day. Could it not more likely have been that God or His chosen scribe used the term day to denote a separate interval or period of time rather than the time interval in which the earth makes one full revolution on its axis? Remember, this account of creation was first written thousands of years before humankind even suspected that the earth rotated or orbited the sun or that the sun was a star like all the rest of the stars in the night sky, so how could God have used language consistent with that future knowledge? God used language that people in the time of Moses would understand.

The second argument, and one that is hotly pursued today, has to do with evolution and intelligent design. Evolution is a theory in which life has evolved through a process called natural selection in which the fittest, strongest characteristics of a species survive and the lesser one is sloughed off.

Look again at the story of creation and please do not get hung up on the time frame. Is it really important to its significance whether creation took place in six days or over several billions of years? It is certainly not important. But back to the biblical account—God did accomplish the entire creation process in a sequence of individual steps, and after each step, God paused and reflected and confirmed that what had been done was good and acceptable. The theory has not yet been proven and accepted as scientific fact, but it has been useful in explaining a number of biological observations. Some find this line of reasoning to be offensive since it seems to imply that humankind evolved naturally from some previous life-form, the most commonly selected being apes. The Bible clearly states that God created man in God's image as a separate step in the creation process. These dissenters from evolution thus offer a counterproposal called intelligent design in which it is suggested that God intervened in the natural selection process to interject humankind as a fully developed and separate species. First of all, such a proposal is not inconsistent with the creation story, but rather it is completely consistent. The entire process of creation took place in a series of steps. One of these steps, and the last, was the creation of "man." So is not the proposal of intelligent design reasonable? Yes, except that the scientific community does not like to interject God or God's actions into explanatory reasoning, thus the rejection of God as the Creator. I find myself riding the fence on this intelligent design issue. Is it possible that God intervened specifically to create humankind? Of course, God as Creator can intervene at any time God wants in the ways and events of the "world" that God created. But for a moment, let's look at this from God's viewpoint. Since God knows the future as well as the present and past, in planning creation, God could foresee the ultimate outcome before setting the process into play and, if necessary, make those changes required for the process to produce "man in His image" through natural selection. So, again, what difference does it make? Maybe in years to come, science will discover evidence to better answer this question. As for evolution, where it is useful, continue to use it. Where it fails, modify or reject it. It's still a theory.

Before we leave God in creation, I want to reemphasize one critical point. If we accept God as the Creator, we have defined the foundation of our relationship with God, our faith. God made everything that we know or can know in this world in which we live, including ourselves. Our relationship with God then must be one of unending thanks, unceasing adoration, and immeasurable love. If not for God, we wouldn't exist. Our inherent vanity should force us to fall to our knees and worship our creator God.

God Speaks

The kind of questions that dog people in the quiet of the night—even people who believe in God, in the Christian, triune God, or, maybe, especially these people—include "How good must I be in order to get into heaven?" "Where and what is heaven?" "How much must I give?" "How am I supposed to love my enemy? I don't even like Mabel Schultz, and she hasn't done anything bad to me, except for her bad breath!" and a thousand other such questions. You'd like to have answers. In fact, you really need answers in order to better understand your relationship to God, but where do you find them?

If I were to say to you, "How about the Bible?" you'd probably answer, "I've tried that, but all I find is a bunch of archaic lingo about things that have no place in our world today. What does it say in the Bible about whether stem cell research is okay or not? You know, what I'd really like—it sounds pretty silly—but what I'd really like would be to sit at God's feet and have Him tell me these things, and I could ask questions if I didn't understand. That's what I'd really like, but that's pretty ridiculous, huh?"

Well, the "ask questions" part might be a bit difficult, but the "sit at the feet" part isn't so unreasonable. That's exactly what the apostles did. For two or three years, they lived with Jesus and listened to Him and asked questions and sat at His feet, and in the four gospels, we have a pretty complete record of what Jesus told them. "Yes, but that's Jesus. I said God!"

Oh, you mean that guy in a long white robe with white hair and beard, sitting on a cloud. You need to know that really isn't God at all. God isn't a physical person. God is a spirit, and we really have no idea what a spirit looks like, or if spirits are visible to humans or any other living entities. That's exactly why God sent Jesus into the world, so that we would have a humanlike person to tell us about God and what's expected of us and what we all can expect in return. And if you'll remember, Jesus is not just a messenger from God. Jesus is God—God the Son, one with the Father—so when Jesus tells us something, we are hearing directly from God, not from a messenger or prophet. Don't feel bad about this ambiguity about Jesus. The apostles, who had lived with Him for several years, had the same problem. Just before Jesus was betrayed, He was speaking to the apostles, and Philip asked Him to show them the Father so that they would understand (John 14:8–10). Jesus replied that He and the Father are one. "Whoever has seen me has seen the Father. The words that I say to you I do not speak on my own; but the Father who dwells in me does his works."

We cannot have, nor should we need, any clearer affirmation than that. When Jesus speaks, we are hearing, directly, God speaking. What then about all the rest of the Bible, the nearly eight hundred pages of the Old Testament and the rest of the New Testament? Do we just ignore them because they aren't God's direct words? Not at all. They are clearly God speaking to us through different, and mostly indirect, channels. There are a number of examples in the Old Testament of God speaking directly to humans. God spoke to Moses on several occasions—when the Israelites needed food and water and when God gave them the Ten Commandments. God spoke to Abraham when God promised him a son and when God demanded that son in sacrifice to test Abraham's faith. God talked to Saul and to Job and to Lot. God spoke to a number of people, but in each such instance, God had some specific, important point to make or task to accomplish in His long and torturous attempt to establish the proper relationship between Himself and humankind. And that really is what the Old Testament is about—the account of God's continued help for us and attempts to reach a loving and respectful relationship with us and of our failure to respond in a loving and respectful manner.

However, don't look at this as a failure in God's plans, because God knew from the beginning, from Adam and Eve, how we humans would respond. This long and tortuous process, however, was necessary to make it absolutely clear to us that there is no possible way that we humans are going to live pure lives, perfectly obeying a set of laws of behavior, even those set down by God. So where does Jesus fit into this scheme of things? He is not God's final desperate attempt to bail out the Israelites. No, Jesus is the Messiah, planned from the beginning, from before the creation of "our world" as we know it. He tells us Himself, "Do not think that I have come to abolish the law or the prophets; I have come not to abolish but to fulfill" (Matthew 5:17). Jesus is not an afterthought. Jesus is the proof of God's plan, the evidence of what a perfect human is, the example of what God wants us to be. He is a human so that we can experience, understand, and emulate Him. But God also knew what the general human reaction would be to Jesus—that our self-centeredness would ultimately force us to reject Him but that through Jesus's perfect example, Jesus who first of all is God, we would recognize that we humans are incapable of the sinless behavior that is God's alone. Those who killed Jesus's human form could not believe that He came from God and that He is in fact God! So they tried to eliminate Him—they had Him crucified in a way that showed clearly that He was dead. God, however, had other plans. To prove that God was still in control and that Jesus is truly God, He raised Jesus from the tomb, allowed Him to be seen and touched by a number of people, and then brought Him back to heaven. Matthew 5:18–19 might seem to diminish the welcoming tenderness of the new covenant under Jesus when He goes on to say, "For truly I tell you, until heaven and earth pass away, not one letter, not one stroke of a letter, will pass from a law until all is accomplished. Therefore, whoever breaks one of the least of these commandments, and teaches others to do the same, will be called least in the kingdom of heaven; but whoever does them and teaches them will be called great in the kingdom of heaven."

We are taught that through belief in Jesus's divinity, we are ensured of forgiveness through confession of those sins that we, as humans, are incapable of escaping and are blessed with eternal life. Where exactly did Jesus say that? It's wonderful news, but have we arrived at that assurance through wishful thinking, or did Jesus actually tell us so?

His claim about "coming to fulfill" goes on to state that the law remains in effect in all its detail.

This is titled "God Speaks," and the case has been made to restrict that essentially to God the Son, Jesus. Before we do that, however, there are questions for the Christian about what importance and relevance we give to the words of God the Father, particularly in the Old Testament. As I discovered on reexamination, the Father had a great deal to say to us humans, especially in the first five books of the Bible, the Jewish Torah. Do they have the same meaning and importance for us today?

God and the Legends

The American Heritage Dictionary defines "legend" as "an unverified popular story handed down from earlier times." I chose legends because this term seems to me best to describe the events and people that are involved in the remainder of Genesis, following the creation, and the early part of Exodus. That the stories written here are unverified is obvious. Even the existence of the specific men and women described goes beyond historic record. Some of the essential ingredients of the earlier stories seem to defy today's common and scientific knowledge. But they are part of God's story, using picturesque and allegorical language, important to disclose some aspect of God's nature and relationship with humankind. At first, I thought to call this "God and the Patriarchs," but that term usually is confined to Abraham, Isaac, and Jacob and might have excluded critical elements such as Adam, Eve, and Noah, among others. At first, I vacillated over whether to include Adam and Eve here or in the discussion of the creation, but since the journey we are about to start deals with God's relationship with humankind, I felt they should be included here.

We'll start with Adam and Eve in the garden of Eden (Genesis 3). Whether you believe that every statement in this chapter is literally true or whether you accept it as an allegorical description of God's relationship with early humans is immaterial. What is important is what it tells us about God and about us. First of all, it tells us something basic and intrinsic of human nature—that we are self-serving, that selfish actions will always surface in human relations, and that unqualified love, other than self-love, will always fall short. That's what Eve and the apple show us. Here, there doesn't seem even to be any great and compelling need that caused Eve to disobey God's wishes, just simple curiosity. Again, God's disappointment seems staged. He had to know, as He knows everything, that this would happen, that His admonition to Adam, and supposedly through him to Eve, "of the tree of the knowledge of good and evil you shall not eat," would be disobeyed. God made us, and He had to know our nature. I feel certain that this story simply sets the beginning of God's long and arduous process of teaching the Israelites and us that we, by ourselves, are hopeless and helpless in attempting perfectly to satisfy God's expectations for us.

What does the garden of Eden story tell us about God? His establishing a close and intimate relationship with earliest humankind simply reemphasizes that we humans have been an integral part of God's creation plan from the beginning. When you consider the vastness of what God created and the insignificance of the earth and, certainly, of human life upon it, we should be filled with indescribable awe and pride, exceeded only by our humility and shame at having so often failed to satisfy God's hopes and expectations for us! For humans, this self-interest is like an addiction, except that it's part of our God-given nature. For drug or alcohol addiction, the cause is acquired, and there is no cure, only rehabilitation and support. Human self-interest is much the same, only the cause is built-in, not acquired, and is always in danger of reemerging. God knows this, has always known this—He made us this way. He gave us free will. For us "normal" humans, the only treatment available is to realize the hopelessness of our situation and then to turn our lives over to God and pray. God is our only hope, and it is through His mercy that that hope is realized. So what are the lessons to be learned from the garden of Eden story? First, God has a key role for us to play in His scheme of things. Second, without God's mercy and love, we are helpless to fulfill God's plans for us.

The next recorded interaction of God and humans is the story of Cain and Abel (Genesis 4). This is another of those early Bible accounts where it isn't good to get too involved in the details. It's never been clear to me why God rejected Cain's offering and accepted Abel's. There seems no indication that either was offered with more devotion and sincerity than the other, yet God accepted one and rejected the other. I've read several commentaries, which only served to reinforce my conviction that there are times when it's better to ignore the details since the commentaries involved speculation at best. Regardless, God's apparent favoritism to Abel moved Cain to jealousy and led to the first incidence of murder mentioned in the Bible. It seems that there must have been some pretty intense competition for God's approval and affection between Cain and Abel to have produced such a gross action by Cain. God's reaction clearly shows that, at least at this point in His relationship with the people of earth, He was inclined to judge and to punish. This will be shown again and again throughout the Old Testament—it's done to make it crystal clear to us that until we accept and admit that we are inherently incapable of reaching on our own the level of perfection in our lives expected by God and turn to Him humbly for help, our salvation is not possible. But that's the story of the New Testament.

One small aside that may be worth mentioning at this point—in Genesis 1 and 2, it is made clear that Adam and Eve are the first two humans, both created by the direct intervention of God, and there is no indication that God intervened further in the creation of human life until the birth of Christ. Thus, by inference, all further human life must have derived from the union of Adam and Eve by natural reproduction. However, when Cain was expelled by God, he went to the land of Nod, east of Eden, and there found himself a wife, because in Genesis 4:17, it says, "Cain knew his wife, and she conceived and bore Enoch." I mention this only as further justification for considering this early biblical language as allegory rather than historic fact; otherwise, his wife could only have been his sister.

The next significant event involving God and people on earth is Noah and the ark (Genesis 6–9). I find myself unable to treat this whole account as anything other than allegory. Aside from the problems of a few men (Noah and his three sons) being able to build a boat of cedar five hundred feet long by eighty-five feet wide by fifty feet high and fill it with two of every species of animal, bird, and insect collected from the farthest reaches of the earth with enough food to sustain him, his family, and all these menagerie for somewhere between 150 days and seven months, there is an even larger question regarding the flood itself. The purpose of the flood is because God decides no longer to tolerate the "wickedness of humankind." He is going to mount a flood that will cover the entire surface of the earth to a level twenty-five feet above the highest mountains, thus killing every living thing except those safely contained in the ark. Now let me tell you, that's one humongous amount of water! In fact, according to Wikipedia, if all the water, vapor, clouds, and ice in earth's atmosphere were to be condensed, it would add about one inch of water over the entire surface of the earth. One inch! Just a bit short of the six miles or so deep of water needed to cover the highest mountains. So much for the flood. That leaves me with two options. One, I can say, "That's God stuff and I know that God made our universe and is all-powerful, so if God says it happened, it did." Or I can say, "That's allegory. God is using picturesque language to tell us something, and I've got to try to figure out what it is." As I said, I've chosen the latter.

The question now is, What is God telling us in the story of Noah and the ark? Is it intended "to put the fear of God into us"? In a way, I think so. It certainly reemphasizes that God is completely in control and is capable of dealing with humankind in any way He chooses, including wiping them from the face of the earth if it is His decision "because of their evil nature." Also, it shows again God's selection of a few good people on which to concentrate His close relationship—another step on the way to the "chosen people of Israel." Again and again, God feels compelled to remind us of His position relative to us, and unfortunately, we continue to demonstrate our inability to understand this fact.

The next person of note was Abram, who God later renamed Abraham and upon whom He based His "chosen people." All of Israel claims descent from him, as well as do those of Islamic faith. Why did God chose a select group of people and concentrate His actions and efforts on this special tribe or family? Through Christ, clearly, He extended His mercy and love to all people, Gentiles, and Jews. Why throughout the times of the Old Testament then did God confine His attention to the Israelites? We don't know, but there is one factor that seems compelling. It seems evident that God wanted a record of His interactions with humans to be preserved and eventually written as a history, inspiration, and guide to future generations. That's where the Jews got the Torah and our Bible. Had God spread His encounters around to various people and various areas, it seems unlikely that such records would have been kept or accumulated.

Abram was born in the land of Ur, which archeology has established as a major urban settlement in Mesopotamia in the valley of the Tigris and Euphrates rivers in the third and fourth millennia BC. He moved first with his wife, Sarai (later Sarah), and his father and other members of his family entourage to Haran in northern Mesopotamia and then, at God's direction, to Canaan. There are three events of major importance that significantly involved God during the remainder of Abram's life. The first of these was God's promise to him after settling in Canaan, that "for all of the land that you see I will give to you and your offspring forever. I will make your offspring like the dust of the earth" (Genesis 13:15–16). Thus, God established His chosen people, the descendants of Abraham, promising that He and they would have this everlasting relationship of respect and love and that the land that they then occupied would be theirs for all time. Later God amplified this description of their land to include everything from the "river of Egypt to the great river, the river Euphrates" (Genesis 15:18–21), far more expansive than the original definition of what Abraham "could see" from where he was standing in Canaan and certainly larger than now occupied by the nation of Israel. In a sense, God laid down in prehistory the foundation for the strife and hatred that exist in the Near East today between the Arab world and Israel.

Abraham believed and accepted God's word in faith, but even his faith was stretched in the face of his and Sarah's age. Abraham was near a hundred and Sarah near ninety. It could be a bit difficult to accept that their offspring was going to populate several nations when they were childless at that age. In fact, Abraham several times humbly directed that concern to God, and each time was told, essentially, "in good time." Finally, after several years of waiting, God told Abraham, "You shall be the ancestor of a multitude of nations" (Genesis 17:4), and, "Your wife Sarah shall bear you a son" (Genesis 17:19). Sarah was in the next room and laughed when she heard this, and God asked her why she was laughing. "Is anything too wonderful for the Lord?" He admonished. And less than a year later, Sarah gave birth to a son, and they named him Isaac as God requested.

Several years later, when Isaac was a boy, God decided again to test Abraham's faith and told him to take Isaac to a designated place and to "offer him there as a burnt offering" (Genesis 22:2). Can you imagine your response to such a command? Abraham, however, complied without dissent, but as he was preparing to light the pyre, an angel of the Lord called down from heaven and told him to stop because "now I know that you fear God" (Genesis 22:12) and was instructed to sacrifice a ram instead. What do we learn from the story of Abraham and Sarah? It's all about faith; it could almost be called blind faith. Can you imagine two more startling challenges to one's faith than, first, to be told that your ninety-year-old wife was going to present you with that long-awaited heir and then to be told to sacrifice that son to God without explanation or reason? Abraham's faith was up to the challenge in both instances, which tells us that if we are people of strong faith, God will hear our prayers and respond. And again, it was a lesson for Abraham and us, because God already knew how Abraham would respond and, through faith, Abraham knew that God would not demand Isaac's life. This also tells us that at first glance, God may seem stern and without compassion, but when you look deeper, God never asks of us more than we are capable of giving. The adventures of Abraham also point out the value for us of patience where God is concerned. God's time and our time are two very different things. We simply are incapable of understanding time in an infinite and eternal world. Our physical lives are measured, they have a beginning and an ending, so there's always the pressure of waiting too long, but God knows that our physical lives are insignificant except in how we relate them to Him. If God says, "Wait," then wait, because He knows that you have the time.

Abraham's life could be characterized by one word, obedience—obedience based on love. Abraham had no question about obeying God's requests (commands?). His faith told him that the all-powerful God must be obeyed and that God loved him unconditionally and would make no demands upon him that were not in his best interests. Such faith is to be eternally sought.

Perhaps the biggest difficulty for us in sensing God's presence is knowing if and when God is speaking to us. Abraham had absolutely no question that God was making these demands of him. He knew he was talking to God. How can we know? I have no pat answer, but certainly, getting to know God, getting closer to Him, has to help. Praying and talking to God has to be a big part of it. I've often heard—I'm sure you have too—"God told me to..." or "God wants me to..." Somehow, these people were sure that they had heard directly from God, or at least, they felt strongly that they had. How does this happen? I don't think that I personally have ever heard such a command or felt that God had asked something specific of me. Is it that I'm not listening or not tuned to God's messages? Maybe as we proceed on this journey, at some point we'll find out or maybe it's just that as you get to know God more fully, you reach a point where you know what God wants of you, instinctively. In any case, it's a very relevant question.

The next of the legends, Isaac, does not appear as "newsworthy" as either his predecessor or successor, but there's no question that he is key in God's plan for the "chosen people." Isaac is the long-promised son for Abraham, through whom the nation of Israel will be created and through whom, ultimately, God's love and mercy will be extended to the entire world.

Part 1

How God Became King: The Forgotten Story of the Gospels

In this book, the author presents compelling arguments asserting that the church and biblical scholars over the past several centuries have completely missed the essence of the gospel writings, specifically the canonic gospels of Matthew, Mark, Luke, and John, which are included at the beginning of all Christian bibles. The impact of his position is that because of this "misreading," the established church universally fails to recognize one of the most fundamental and critical teachings of the New Testament and of the Christian faith—not only did Christ atone for human sins through His crucifixion, resurrection, and ascension, but also through these same events, Christ inaugurated *God's kingdom here one earth*! We are in it, in the midst of it, and if that is true, it has some significant implications for how we approach worship and how we lead our lives.

In what follows, I will try to summarize accurately Bishop Wright's analyses and arguments as I understand them. I am not a theologian, nor am I formally trained in any aspect of religious thought and teaching. I am a lifelong Christian, participating actively in church worship services and lay activities. Since my retirement, I have spent much more time in reading and discussing religion and the Bible.

3

My exposure to *How God Became King* was through a study course in my local congregation that involved reading chapter after chapter, followed by weekly group discussion. You will rightly assume that I was impressed and moved by what I learned. I am now rereading the book, more slowly and thoughtfully, with the benefit of our group discussions. I will present my summary chapter by chapter and hope that it retains the essence of Bishop Wright's thoughts on this important matter, but I would never suggest that it could in any way stand in place of his beautifully and eloquently presented scholarly writings. In addition to my summary, as appropriate, I will include in each chapter such personal "thoughts" that have occurred to me or points that came up during our group discussion relative to Bishop Wright's formal presentation.

Preface

The author wastes no time in setting the stage for his ensuing discussion. "Most of the Western Christian tradition has simply forgotten what the gospels are really all about." He goes on to say "that what we need is not just a bit of fine-tuning, but that we need a fundamental rethink about what the gospels are trying to say and not least about how we then might order our life and work in accordance with them" (Wright, N. T., *How God Became King: The Forgotten Story of the Gospels* [New York: Harper One, an imprint of Harper Collins Publishers, 2016]). He then very simply unveils his basic premise as disclosed in the title of this work, that Jesus, through His birth, life, crucifixion, resurrection, and ascension, initiated God's kingdom here on earth two thousand years ago and that now His kingdom is moving forward in and through Christ's followers. The author wonders what would happen to the church's mission and unity if we all accepted that as what the gospels are really telling us.

Wright goes on to acknowledge that accepting God as king here on earth might be unsettling to many Christians as well as non-Christians. Doesn't this rather smack that dreaded word "theocracy"? And if God is king here, now why do we still have all the dreadful criminal acts and diseases happening as well as starvation and wars and natural disasters? All valid questions, but questions that must be dealt with after we have first heard and either accepted or rejected the arguments for the basic premise.

Bishop Wright then outlines the approach that he will follow in his book. In part 1, he details the problem, the fact that the gospels have been misread and misinterpreted by theologians and biblical scholars. In part 2, he will "explore four dimensions of the canonical gospels that, again, have normally been screened out in modern Western readings and that we need to recover if we are to allow the gospels to tell us the story they intend to tell." Then in "Part III," the author explores "how the two vital themes so often separated, the kingdom and the cross, come together in the gospels, knock sparks off each other, and reinforce each other in setting out a claim that today's church has all but forgotten a claim as much in what we call the political as in what we call the religious or spiritual sphere." This is the crux of his argument. Finally, in part 4, he covers some of the implications of this new interpretation and attitude toward the gospels. The "Introduction" details the explanation of why and how he came to write this book and concludes with his acknowledging those who helped and contributed to its publication.

The Empty Cloak

Chapter 1

THE MISSING MIDDLE

To begin his discussion, Bishop Wright has selected a title for part 1 that emphasizes the critical omission in the church's definition of Christian faith occasioned by its teachings and historic creeds. "The Empty Cloak" strongly suggests that the "appearance" of the church, all that is seen in the world today, excludes or omits a critical element of its real and intended essence. This does not mean that what is seen is not of vast importance or that it falsely represents what the church is about. Rather it suggests that what is seen today as the belief and meaning of the church is critically incomplete, that it omits a transforming aspect of the church's nature that was passionately believed and strongly intended for inclusion by the founders of the church, the apostles themselves, as was presented and discussed in the gospels.

Wright introduces the problem in chapter 1, first, by describing a personal experience as a teenage boy. In high school, he and some friends in a Christian Studies group were organizing a series of studies about Jesus highlighted by the word "Why." Why was Jesus born? Why did Jesus live? Why did Jesus die? Why did Jesus rise again? Individual boys were each assigned one of the topics for presentation and discussion, and he drew "Why did Jesus live?" Much to his chagrin, the other boys had no trouble finding plenty of helpful information—church tradition, Christ's birth, Christmas, Holy Week, and Easter and whole books written on these subjects and their meaning and significance, emphasizing the virgin birth, Christ's divinity, His atoning for our sins through His crucifixion, resurrection, and ascension. But for the time between his birth and death, there was extraordinarily little to say other than that through His life He set an example of how people should live, and He illustrated these same principles in the stories (parables) He told.

He cured people of their illnesses and afflictions. The "bit between the stable and the cross" is ignored in our statements of faith, the historic creeds, which define our Christian belief. "Does it matter that He did all those things, that He said all those things, that He was all those things? Would it have made any difference if, as the virgin-born Son of God, He had been plucked from total obscurity and crucified, dying for our sins, without any of that happening? If not, why not?" And there seemed truly little available to help him answer the question, "Why did Jesus live?" That was the dilemma he faced.

About fifteen years later, after he had committed his life to God with emphasis on study and teaching, the author had another experience that reemphasized and began to focus his attention and thinking on this same problem. He was asked to give a Bible exposition to the student

Christian Union at Cambridge with the title "the Gospel in the Gospels." This request presupposed the term "the gospel" to mean "the message: the good news that, because of Jesus's death alone, your sins can be forgiven, and all you have to do is believe it, rather than trying to impress God with doing good works." A great deal is said about "the gospel" in this sense. In Paul's letter to the Romans, it appears the whole letter has been directed toward the goal of showing that God demands our action, as well as our believing and thinking. However, essentially nothing appears in "the gospels" of Matthew, Mark, Luke, and John on these subjects. "Atonement" and "justification by faith" may be implied in the gospels simply because they each tell the story of the death of Jesus, but to find "the gospel" in them is a different matter. The author doesn't tell us how he approached this problem in the lecture that which he delivered at Cambridge but uses the incident only to demonstrate further how the church, in developing these two of its most fundamental tenets of faith, has essentially ignored the gospels, the "on-site" reports of Jesus's life, what He did and what He said, and what the "face-to-face" reporters understood it to mean. As Wright says, "It doesn't look as though the gospels really make 'atonement,' in the sense the church has come to see that word, their main theme."

One more personal experience is cited to illustrate the problem. Twenty-five years later, in a discussion with "a well-known Christian leader from another continent," Wright was expressing his concern that the gospels had— "As it were, fallen off the canon of the New Testament as far as many Christians were concerned. Matthew, Mark, Luke, and John were used to support points you might get out of

Paul, but their actual message had not been glimpsed, let alone integrated into the larger biblical theology in which they claimed to belong. This, I remember saying, was heavily ironic in a tradition (to which he and I both belonged) that prided itself on being 'biblical'." At the end of that conversation, his friend wondered if he was being told that he was insufficiently biblical. Wright goes on to say, "Yes, I replied. That is exactly what I am saying. And if that was true of him, it is true of a great deal of the Western Christian tradition: Catholic and Protestant, liberal and evangelical, charismatic, and contemplative. We use the gospels. We read them aloud in worship. We often preach from them. But have we even begun to hear what they are saying, the whole message, which is so much greater than the sum of the small parts with which we are, on one level, so familiar? I do not think so. This is the lifetime puzzle. It is not just that we have all misread the gospels, though I think that is broadly true. It is more that we have not really read them at all. We have fitted them into the framework of ideas and beliefs that we have acquired from other sources. I want in this book to allow them, as far as I can, to speak for themselves. Not everyone will like the result."

Bishop Wright goes on to examine the striking differences between the gospels and the creeds. He says, "The problem about the puzzling relationship between 'the gospel' and 'the gospels' is reflected in the equally puzzling relationship between the gospels and the great Christian creeds." The problem is that the creeds, the Apostles' Creed, the Nicene Creed, and even the Athanasian Creed, take us in our statement of faith, directly from Christ's birth to his death, resurrection, and ascension, completely ignoring the majority of Jesus's life and ministry that, in fact, constitutes the bulk of all four gospels. The author maintains that the gospels "tell us about what we might call his kingdom-inaugurating work: the deeds and words that declared that God's kingdom was coming then and there, in some sense or other, on earth as in heaven. They tell us a great deal about that, but the great creeds don't." There follows a lengthy discussion of why the historic creeds were formulated in the first place. In the first centuries of its existence, the church was beset by a number of conflicting opinions regarding several aspects of Christian belief. Was Christ truly divine or just a particularly good and moral man? Was he really the promised messiah? Was salvation "bought" for us through the sacrifice of Jesus or only through personal achievement of lofty spiritual enlightenment—Arianism and Gnosticism and others? To obviate these heretical movements, the leaders and scholars formulated the creeds as statements of belief and faith, as the bedrock definitions of the Christian faith. Wright does not in any sense attack or demean the creeds or their value and importance. He does, however, lament the fact that the church has over the centuries allowed the creeds to define the limits of our faith in such a way as to effectively downplay the role that the gospels should play in our understanding of the timing of the establishment of God's kingdom here on earth. If his assessment of this problem is accurate and correct, this is certainly a grievous oversight and one that needs seriously to be remedied.

The author follows this with a detailed examination of both the Apostles' Creed and the Nicene Creed to demonstrate the oversight. In the first of these, we go from "conceived" and "born" directly to "suffered, crucified, dead and buried" without any mention of His life or ministry. The Nicene Creed spends more time defining the nature of Christ, His divinity and relation to God, but moves quickly from "was made man" to "crucified," "suffered and was buried," without any suggestion of the meaning of His life.

> There is nothing about what Jesus did, or why he did it, or how anything he did relates either to his birth or his death. There is, in short, an enormous gap." "What they (the gospels) do say makes the problem a lot more acute. The gospels speak a great deal, as we shall see, about the 'kingdom of God' as, in some sense or other, a present reality in the ministry of Jesus. This, indeed, is at the heart of what we need to explore in this book. But not only do the creeds fail to mention this in connection with Jesus's life (or indeed with his birth or his death). The Nicene Creed implies, to the contrary, that Jesus's 'kingdom' will be established only when he 'comes again in glory': 'He will come again in glory to judge the living and the dead, and his kingdom shall have no end.' It doesn't actually say that his kingdom will only be set up at that point, but the sequence of clauses gives that clear impression.

Bishop Wright goes on to discuss the significance of Jesus's ascension that is described in both creeds along with the statement "seated at the right hand of the Father" and that, according to the author, could only be interpreted in ancient Jewish thought to mean that at "that moment Jesus was the Father's right-hand man, in charge of the entire world. But in our own day the 'ascension' is just a way of saying that Jesus 'went to heaven when he died'" where he assumed an honored position at God's right hand. "In fact, the ascension, for many people, implies Jesus's absence, not his universal presence and sovereign rule."

However, the gospels present a quite different picture of the kingdom. As the author states, "But for the four gospels this wasn't something that simply began at the ascension. It was true, in a sense, from the moment Jesus began his public career. This was what they were trying to tell us. And most Christians have never even thought about such a thing, let alone begun to figure out what it means for us today. This is the problem, I believe, with the great majestic creeds, full as they are of solemn truth and supple wisdom. They manage not to mention the main thing the gospels are trying to tell us, and they talk about something else instead. Ought we to be worried by this? Are we missing something?"

Wright follows this with a lengthy discussion of how all this might have come about. The creeds resulted from a need to answer and put down the various controversial interpretations that arose during the early church's formation. Since there is little evidence of controversial thinking about God's kingdom on earth, it was not a subject of discussion at the councils that were held to formulate the creeds. Over the following centuries, since there was no authoritative statement from the church concerning the kingdom, it got overlooked as thinking and teachings developed. The gospels assumed a place in the liturgy and preaching of the church, but their basic message and meaning was ignored. "What I see, in other words, is a great gulf opening up between the canon and the creeds. The canonical gospels give us a Jesus whose public career radically mattered as part of his overall accomplishment, which had to do with the kingdom of God. The creeds give us a Jesus whose miraculous birth and saving death, resurrection and ascension are all we need to know."

The chapter concludes with a discussion of a popular theological trend in the twentieth century that concentrated all attention on the cross and looked on individual incidents in the gospels as stories, often mythological, told as "expressions of early Christian experience projected back onto the fictive (fictional) screen of the history of Jesus." Rudolph Bultmann, a German Lutheran scholar, originated this thinking and successfully influenced many scholars and students of the past century. It is not hard to see what effect this would have on attempts to push forward Wright's position.

Chapter 2

THE OPPOSITE PROBLEM: ALL BODY, NO CLOAK

The discussion now switches to those "believers" (or are they nonbelievers) who place total emphasis on the nature and activities of Jesus's life and deny His divinity. Wright states it thus,

> Ever since the eighteenth century it has been fashionable to come at the gospels by asking the historical question: Did it really happen? And the answer that the intellectual fashions of our skeptical age have demanded has been something like this. Yes, Jesus really existed, but all that material around the edge—his miraculous birth, the saving meaning of his death, and above all his resurrection and ascension—never happened. That is what the later church added to express its own faith.

But when we take that away, the bit in the middle that we are left with—the body without the cloak, if you like—is a quite different story from the one the church has told. Take away the beginning and the ending, the bits you find in the creeds, the bits that people refer to today when they talk about 'preaching the gospel,' and the Jesus you are left with is one of three things. Either he is a revolutionary, hoping to overthrow the Romans by military violence and establish a new Jewish state. Or he is a wild-eyed apocalyptic visionary, expecting the end of the world. Or he is a mild-mannered teacher of sweet reasonableness, of the fatherhood of God and the brotherhood of 'Man.' Or he is some combination of the above. There are plenty of possibilities.

If you accept any of these possibilities, Jesus had to be either deluded, demented, or a charlatan. If there is anything good about this approach, it does produce "a strong 'social gospel' agenda in which many of the things the gospels emphasize about Jesus—his care for the poor, the sick, the weak, and so on—are given a new energy that official 'orthodoxy' has often strangely failed to supply." It is, however, much too lukewarm to represent the major salvation program of an omnipotent, all-loving God.

The author goes on to point out that much good has been done under the guise of this "social gospel" movement. The biggest problem with this approach is that despite the good that it has done, the world remains a wicked, degraded, and corrupt place. As Wright states,

> The problem is that, a century after the "social gospel" was at its high-water mark, the world, including the Western world, still seems to be a place of great wickedness.
>
> Greed and corruption, oppression of the poor, violence and degradation, war and genocide continue unchecked. It is not only the Jesus of popular imagination, then, who expected something dramatic to happen and was disappointed. The "social gospel" may have helped to clean up some slums, to reduce working hours for women and children in factories, and so on. Wonderful. But homelessness and virtual slave labor are still realities in the modern Western world, never mind elsewhere. Has anything really changed? Faced with this puzzle, it is fair to ask: What difference might it make if the "middle" of the gospels was integrated with the outer' bits? What would it be like if the cloak were no longer empty?

Another popular "liberal" reading of the gospels leads its adherents to the position that the creeds present statements defining Jesus's relationship to God that even Jesus did not put forward. To me, such an interpretation can only have arisen from a very shallow examination of the gospels. Jesus didn't harp about "begotten not made" or "being of one substance with the Father," but He clearly wanted His disciples to understand that He is the Son of God and that He had "seen the Father," and the gospels clearly show this when Peter announces that Jesus is the Messiah, the Son of God, and John introduces his gospel with the unambiguous statement that in the beginning, before all worlds existed, the Word (Jesus) was and always will be. How did they learn these things? Obviously from their Master.

Adjusting the Volume

Chapter 3

THE STORY OF ISRAEL

In this chapter, the author begins his explanation of the meaning of the gospels. The point of this book is to show that the church and Bible scholars have over centuries improperly interpreted and taught the full essence of what the gospel authors were telling us. Wright claims that one of the critical and vital objectives of the gospel writers was to explain that the church, today and from its inception, is made up of the beneficiaries of God's covenant with the Israelites, which has been renewed and expanded to include all nations under the new covenant instituted through Christ's birth, life, death, resurrection and ascension, and that God's kingdom here on earth was instituted two thousand years ago through Christ's ministry here on earth. We, all believers, are the renewed Israelites who work in God's kingdom and through whom God's kingdom on earth is developed and extended with the direction and guidance of the Holy Spirit. That has some serious implications for us all.

To present and explain his position, the author compares the reading and understanding of the gospels to listening to a symphony over a stereo sound system that has four speakers. The analogy to a four-speaker sound system is used since Wright suggests that there are four main strands or dimensions inherent in the story that the gospelers are telling. Thus, in a symphony, if each speaker emphasized a different section of the orchestra, for example, strings, brass, woodwinds, and percussion, the composite output of the system would only sound as it should if each speaker had its volume properly adjusted. If not, it would produce something unintended, certainly misleading, or even cacophonous. The four strands or dimensions of the gospels that Wright has chosen are as follows: "the climax of the story of Israel," "the story of Jesus as the story of Israel's God coming back to his people," "reflections of the life of the early church," and "the story of the kingdom of God clashing with the kingdom of Caesar." And he insists that all four canonic gospels are telling the identical story though in different ways and emphasizing different aspects of it. In this and the following three chapters, the author discusses each of these subjects as they are presented in each of the individual gospels. Chapter 4, as its title indicates, deals with "the Story of Israel."

To energize the contention that the gospels are a continuation of the story of Israel as told in the Old Testament, in fact, that they describe the climax of that story, Wright interjects the two terms prequel and sequel as they apply to storytelling in popular literature. He first mentions *the Wonderful Wizard of Oz* by L. Frank Baum, published in 1900, and *Wicked* by Gregory Maguire, published in 1995.

The second book tells of the history of Oz, which adds meaning to the later story of Dorothy's visit, published earlier. He next describes a comparable situation relating to J. R. R. Tolkien's *the Hobbit* (1937) and *the Lord of the Rings* (1954–1955) followed later by Tolkien's son, Christopher, with *Silmarillion* (1977) and twelve-volume *History of Middle-earth* (1983–1996) in which the scene of Tolkien's original works was explained and enlarged in significance. The relationship between the Old Testament and gospels is similar in that they represent a continuum, but dissimilar since there is no question that the Old Testament writings predate the gospels. The problem that does exist is that much church teaching ignores the Old Testament and its teachings, except to prophecy the Messiah, and bases its whole substance on Christ's teachings. The gospels are not a continuation of the story of Israel, nor its climax, but the gospels are all that really matter. "The first speaker of our quadraphonic sound system (that needs) to be turned up is this: the four gospels present themselves as the climax of the story of Israel. All four evangelists, I suggest, deliberately frame their material in such a way as to make this clear, though many generations of Christian readers have turned down the speaker to such an extent that they have been able, in effect, to ignore it."

He continues with a discussion of "the strange story of Israel." When you read the Old Testament, you are left with the feeling that "this story is supposed to be going somewhere; but that it hasn't gotten there yet. It is an unfinished narrative, an unfinished agenda. Things are supposed to happen that haven't happened yet." You have the feeling that it has "great beginnings and wonderful visions of God's plan and purposes, then a steady decline and puzzling and shameful multiple failures, all ending in a question mark." "The problem is that we have all read the gospels if we haven't been careful, simply as God's answer to the plight of humans in general. The implied backstory hasn't been the story of Abraham, of Moses, of David, of the prophets; it's been the story of Adam and Eve, of 'Everyman,' sinning and dying and needing to be redeemed." The story of Israel itself has been quietly left aside. But God did begin His continuing relationship with humankind by selecting Abraham and his descendants as "His people" and promised to stay with them through all time. The gospels tell, "The story of Jesus is the story in which that long history, warts and all, reaches its God-ordained climax." So this first speaker in our sound system must be turned much louder than most people expect.

In the rest of this chapter, the author centers on each of the gospels, individually, to show how that writer is telling this same story. He turns first to Matthew, who—before telling one word about the life of Jesus—gives a detailed genealogy for the Messiah, the son of David, the son of Abraham. Why? It clearly shows that not only is Jesus part of that story of God and Israel, but also it establishes—and the author goes to great lengths to support this point—that to a Jew of that time, two thousand years ago, the timing of Jesus's birth and life would have complied with what the Prophet Daniel predicted for the end of the exile and the coming of the Messiah. This was the hope of Jewish people at that time, that the exile would finally end and that God would return to them as He had promised and live with them as He had during the exodus and establishing of

Israel as a nation, and when this happens, it would be "the time of real, utter, and lasting freedom. That is the hope that sustained the Israelites in the long years of the centuries before the time of Jesus."

Thoughts

In the next section titled "the Hidden Underlying Challenge: Theocracy," Bishop Wright, I feel, overstates the problem. To quote, "When we examine the wider movements of thought and culture in the eighteenth century, we find something of enormous significance for understanding why the gospels were being read in the way they were. At the heart of 'the Enlightenment' was a resolute determination that 'God'—whoever 'God' might be—should no longer be allowed to interfere, either directly or through those who claimed to be his spokespeople, in the affairs of this world. Once 'man had come of age,' there' was no room for theocracy. It was as simple as that. God was pushed upstairs, like the doddering old boss who used to run the company but has now been superseded. He has, no doubt, a notional place of 'honor,' a cozy office where he can sit and imagine he is still in charge. But nobody is fooled. The new generation is running the business now. They know it, and his supporters had better get used to it. Thus, for the European and American Enlightenment, God was superannuated to a position of totally ineffectual 'honor'."

I can understand how one might take advantage of the "separation of church and state" to depress or subvert religious practices or even to deny the existence of God, but to some extent such a statement as quoted above tends to ignore the very abuse that many early American settlers came to this land to escape and thus had a very real abhorrence of it's being reestablished in this country. Theocracy is okay if it is your theocracy, but if it is their theocracy, no way! Think about this—the Islamic population in this country is on a rapid rise. Sometime in the not-too-distant future, Islamic voters could hold a majority in America. How would you like Shariah law? There is already such pressure in some parts of Europe. Freedom of religion is as essential as any other freedom. I cannot believe that even God would want us legislated into being believers. Didn't Jesus Himself espouse such when He said, "Render unto Caesar"? Even if Christ initiated God's kingdom here on earth two thousand years ago, it certainly is not yet in its final form! When it is, it will be theocracy, and that is what we should all be working toward. But until that time, we all may be better able to do that under the umbrella of separation of church and state.

Now I will get off my soapbox.

Revelation

The book of Revelation was written at the time when Christians were entering a time of persecution. Roman authorities were beginning to enforce the cult of emperor worship and Christians were facing increasing hostility.

The purpose of the book was to encourage the faithful to staunchly resist the demands of emperor worship. John informs his readers that the final showdown is imminent. You may notice the distinctive feature in the book of Revelation is prevalent use of the number seven. It appears 52 times which symbolizes completeness.

Prologue:

It has been held that John the Apostle, the son of Zebedee is the author of the book of Revelation. Chapter 1 is a prologue explaining that God's angel appeared to John on the island of Patmos. He was instructed to "write on a scroll of what you see and send it to the seven churches." It further explains that what he saw was the Word of God and the testimony of Jesus Christ.

Chapter 2: To the Church in Ephesus

To the angel of the church in Ephesus write: Doing well except, "I have this against you, that you have abandoned the love that you had at first. Remember then from where you have fallen, repent, and do the works that you did at first. If not, I will come to you and remove your lampstand from its place."

To the Church in Smyrna

You are about to experience tribulation and some will be sent to prison. "Be faithful unto death, and I will give you the crown of life. He who has an ear let him hear."

To the Church in Pergamum

Generally doing well, "But I have a few things against you."

Some hold to the teaching of Balaam. Also some hold to the teachings of the Nicolaitans. Therefore, repent.

To the Church in Thyatira

Very good, except some of you "tolerate that woman Jezebel," sexual immortality, eat food sacrificed to idols. Repent, those who have sinned.

The rest of you continue doing well.

Chapter 3: To the Church in Sardis

"I know your works. You have the reputation of being alive, but you are dead. Wake up, and strengthen what remains and is about to die, for I have not found your works complete in the sight of my God."

To the Church in Philadelphia

You are doing as well as you can under the circumstances. "Because you have kept my word about patient endurance, I will keep you from the hour of trial that is coming on the whole world."

To the Church in Laodicea

"I know your works: you are neither cold nor hot. Because you are lukewarm, and neither cold nor hot, I will spit you out of my mouth. For you say, I am rich, I have prospered, and I need nothing, not realizing that you are wretched, pitiable, poor, blind, and naked."

Chapter 4: The Throne in Heaven

"Come up here... At once I was in the Spirit." God on a throne like jasper and carnelian around it twenty-four thrones and on each side four living creatures with six wings full of eyes one a lion one an ox one a man one an eagle everyone praising God

Chapter 5: The Scroll and the Lamb

A scroll with seven seals in the hand of God and no one able to open the seals. The Lamb with seven horns and seven eyes could open it, and four living creatures and twenty-four elders fell down and sang praises to the Lamb and myriads of angels thousands of thousands sang praises and every creature in heaven and on earth and under the earth and in the sea sang praises to him who sits on the throne and to the lamb

Chapter 6: The Seven Seals

[The first seal] Now I watched when the Lamb opened one of the seven seals, and I heard one of the living creatures say with a voice like thunder, "Come!" and I looked, and behold "a white horse rider given a bow and crown came out to conquer"

[The second seal] A bright red horse rider had a great sword permitted to take peace from earth so people could slay each other.

[The third seal] A black horse rider had a pair of scales "A quart of wheat for a denarius and three quarts of barley for a denarius and do not harm the oil and the wine."

[The fourth seal] A pale horse rider was Death followed by Hades given authority to kill a fourth of the earth.

[The fifth seal] Under the altar those who had been slain for the word of God

[The sixth seal] Earthquake, devastation, sun became black, stars fell from the sky, mountains and islands removed, all on earth fear "the end."

Chapter 7: The 144,000 of Israel Sealed

A voice from heaven said to the four angels who had been given the power to harm the earth that they should hold off until "the servants of our God" had been sealed on their foreheads, and 144,000 of Israel, 12,000 from each of the twelve tribes, were sealed.

A Great Multitude from Every Nation became like the blood of a corpse and every living thing in it died. The third angel poured his bowl into the rivers and springs and they became blood.

And the angel in charge of the waters said, "Just are you, O Holy One, who is and who was, for you brought these judgments. For they have shed the blood of saints and prophets, and you have given them blood to drink. It is what they deserve!"

The fourth angel poured his bowl upon the sun and it was allowed to scorch them with fire. The fifth angel poured out his bowl on the throne of the beast and its kingdom was plunged into darkness.

"People gnawed their tongues in anguish and cursed the God of heaven for their pain and sores. They did not repent of their deeds." The sixth angel poured out his bowl on the great river Euphrates and its water dried up, to prepare the way for the kings from the east. And I saw coming out of the mouths of the dragon, of the beast, and of the false prophet, unclean spirits like frogs, for they are demonic spirits to go to the kings of the world to assemble them for battle against God on the great day that is coming, a battle called Armageddon.

The seventh angel poured his bowl into the air, and a loud voice came out of the temple from the throne saying, "It is done!" And there was lightning, peals of thunder and an earthquake greater than ever before, so tremendous that the great city was split into three parts, every island fled and all mountains disappeared and hundred-pound hail balls fell on the people and they cursed God.

Chapter 17: The Great Prostitute and the Beast

Then one of the seven angels who had the seven bowls came to me and said, "Follow me and I will show you the judgment of the great prostitute (Babylon) with whom the kings of the earth have committed sexual immorality, and with the wine of whose sexual immortality the dwellers on earth have become drunk." I was shown the woman arrayed in gold ornaments and jewels sitting on a scarlet beast with seven heads and ten horns. In her hand was a golden cup full of abominations, and on her forehead was written her name, "Babylon the great, mother of prostitutes and of the earth's abominations." When I saw her I marveled greatly but was told not to marvel for the beast I saw was, and is not, and is about to rise from the bottomless pit and go to destruction. There follows a lengthy explanation of the meaning of the seven heads and ten horns ending with "As for the beast that was and is not, it is an eighth but it belongs to the seven." Duh! The beast and its followers will make the prostitute desolate and naked and they will devour her flesh and burn her up with fire, for God has put this into their minds.

Chapter 18: The Fall of Babylon
After this I saw another angel descend from heaven with great authority and the earth was made bright with his glory. He called out with a mighty voice, "Fallen, fallen is Babylon the great! She has

become a dwelling place for demons, a haunt for every unclean bird, a haunt for every unclean and detestable beast. For all nations have drunk of the wine of the passion of her immorality, etc." Another voice from heaven said, "Come out of her, my people, lest you take part in her sins" followed by a lengthy description of Babylon's transgressions and fall and of the unfortunates who bewailed it.

Chapter 19: Rejoicing in Heaven
"Hallelujah! Salvation and power and glory belong to our God, for his judgments are true and just Praise our God, all you his servants, you who fear him, small and great."
The Marriage Supper of the Lamb
And I heard what seemed to be the voice of a great multitude, crying out, "Hallelujah! For the Lord our God reigns. Let us rejoice and exult and give him the glory, for the marriage of the Lamb has come, and his bride has made herself ready." I was overcome with emotion and fell down at the feet of the angel, and he told me not to, for, "I am a fellow servant with you and your brothers who hold to the testimony of Jesus, Worship God." For the testimony of Jesus is the spirit of prophecy.

The Rider on a White Horse

Heaven opened and I saw a white horse and the one on it is called Faithful and True, and in righteousness he judges and makes war and the name by which he is called is The Word of God. The armies of heaven were following him on white horses. On his robe and on his thigh he has a name King of kings and Lord of lords. An angel called out to all of the birds, "Come, gather for the great supper of God, to eat the flesh of kings, captains, mighty men, horses and their riders, of all men born free and slave, great and small." And the beast and the kings of the world and their armies gathered to make war on the one on the white horse and his armies. The beast and the false prophet were captured and thrown alive into the lake of fire that burns with sulfur. And the rest were slain by the sword that came from the common mouth of him who was sitting on the horse, and all the birds were gorged with their flesh.

Chapter 20: The Thousand Years

An angel cane down from heaven with the key to the bottomless pit and a great chain and he seized Satan the devil, bound him, and threw him into the pit and shut and sealed it for a thousand years. After that he must be released for a little while.

Then I saw thrones and seated on them those to whom authority to judge was committed and the souls of those who had died for God and those who had not worshiped the beast or its image or worn the mark came to life and ruled with Christ for the thousand years. The rest of the dead did not come to life until the thousand years were ended. This is the first resurrection. Blessed and holy is the one who shares in the first resurrection. Over such the second death has no power, but they will be priests of God and of Christ, and they will reign with him for a thousand years.

The Defeat of Satan

When the thousand years are over, Satan will be released and he will deceive the nations of the earth, and gather them for battle, numbers like the sands of the sea. They will surround the camp of the saints and the beloved city, but fire came down from heaven and consumed them and the devil was thrown into the lake of fire and sulfur and will be tormented for eternity.

Judgment Before the Great White Throne

Then I saw a great white throne and him who was seated on it. The dead, great and small, were standing before the throne and being judged by what they had done, by what was written in the books, including the book of life. The sea gave up its dead to be judged, as did Death and Hades. After this, Death and Hades were thrown into the lake of fire, which is the second death. Anyone, whose name was not found written in the book of life, was thrown into the lake of fire.

Chapter 21: The New Heaven and the New Earth

Then I saw a new heaven and a new earth, for the first had passed away, and the sea no more. I saw the holy city, the new Jerusalem coming down out of heaven from God. A loud voice from the throne saying, "Behold, the dwelling place of God is with man. He will dwell with them and they will be his people, and God himself will be with them as their God. He will wipe every tear from their eyes, and death shall be no more, neither shall there be mourning, nor crying, nor pain anymore, for the former things have passed away". And the one seated on the throne said, "Behold, I am making all things new. He said he will give water from the spring

of the water of life to the thirsty." The one
who conquers will have this heritage, and
I will be his God and he will be my son.
But as for the cowardly, the faithless, the
detestable, etc., their portion will be in the
lake that burns with fire and sulfur, which
is the second death."

The New Jerusalem

Begins a lengthy description of the
splendor and radiance of the new city,
its majestic size and construction of gold
and jewels and gates of pearl, etc. Nothing
unclean will ever enter it, nor "anyone
who does what is detestable or false," only
those who are written in the Lamb's book
of life.

Chapter 22: The River of Life

The river of the water of life flows
from the throne of God and the Lamb
down the center of the street of the city,
and the tree of life grows on each side. "No
longer will there be anything accursed,
but the throne of God and of the Lamb
will be in it and his servants will worship
him. They will see his face, and his name
will be on their foreheads."

Jesus is coming.

"And behold, I am coming soon.
Blessed is the one who keeps the words of
the prophecy of this book."

Followed by lengthy reminders of the dependence on righteous living to participate in the wonders of these prophecies, and the punishments, if not.

Behold I am coming soon, bringing my recompense with me, to repay everyone for what he has done. I am the Alpha and the Omega, the first and the last, the beginning and the end.

Blessed are those who wash their robes, so that they may have the right to the tree of life and that they may enter the city by the gates. Outside are the dogs and sorcerers and the sexually immoral and murderers and idolaters, and everyone who loves and practices falsehood.

I, Jesus, have sent my angel to testify to you about these things for the churches. I am the root and the descendant of David, the bright morning star.

I warn everyone who hears this prophecy not to add to or take away from the words of this book or they will pay the price.

He who testifies to these things says, "Surely I am coming soon." Amen, Come, Lord Jesus! The grace of the Lord Jesus be with all. Amen.

Spiritual Worlds

There is one question about the spiritual world that rarely gets asked openly but gets pondered silently by many Christians. Since it is where I'm going to spend eternity if I pass the test, I sure wonder where and what heaven and hell are. Both questions are toughies. God has said little about heaven except that when Jesus informed the disciples about the "hereafter," he told them heaven is a beautiful and peaceful place and that in His Father's house are many rooms and that there will be a place for them there. The most extensive description of heaven is in Revelation; but that, like many of the descriptive passages in the Bible, uses picturesque, fanciful, and sometimes even scary language to try to portray the magnificence and other worldliness of heaven.

The one thing we do know is that neither heaven nor hell is anywhere in this natural, material world where we now live and know so well, for God is spirit and thus must live in a different world where everything is both eternal and nonmaterial. Nothing in our material world is eternal, and since we are told that when we go to heaven we will be with God, we must go where He is. We can also say with assurance that there will be no golf courses or idyllic fishing holes or lovely flower gardens to putter around in, since all those earthly things are "heavenly" only by present material standards and thus are subject to decay and deterioration at some point and cannot exist in an eternal, spiritual world. Also, there definitely will not be those "29 beautiful virgins" to lollygag around with, for heaven will certainly be without sex, in form or action. Humans on earth are given sex to ensure procreation and that certainly is not needed in heaven.

Beyond those sorts of things, there is little else about heaven that we know, or probably ever will know, regardless of how far our understanding of quantum physics and superstrings may lead us. Everything that we as humans can ever know and understand is restricted to the things of this material world, which we can sense, describe, and talk about. We certainly cannot sense things that do not and could not even exist in this four-dimensional world in which we live, and our language would simply be incapable of describing them even if we could.

Now I'm going to get really speculative. Saint Paul told us, in 1 Corinthians 15:42–53, that when we go to heaven, we will discard our corruptible bodies for incorruptible ones. As I said above, our present earthly bodies, after we die, will deteriorate, as eventually do all earthly things, animate or inanimate. Oh, some of the archeological finds are thousands of years old and still recognizable, but given enough time they also will waste away; and anyway, compared to eternity, thousands or even millions of years are just a tick of the clock. What does Saint Paul signify by using the words "corruptible" and "incorruptible"? He certainly is referring to the deterioration that our bodies will experience, the rotting and decay that is inevitable. Cremation will avoid those unpleasant-sounding processes, but the ashes that are left simply bypass them and shorten the process. So that's part of what Saint Paul meant. But I think there's a much more important meaning.

If you spend some time examining the nature of sin, I think you will find that all sin is integrally connected to the self-gratification offered through some unseemly or at least unnecessarily urgent aspect of our material world at the expense of one or more other humans. The big and obvious sins like murder, theft, and adultery are easy to see; but even the less obvious like slander, envy, and lust are just first steps before turning into something more obvious. And there are sins of omission and of commission, like passing by a person with obvious needs without stopping to help, and these certainly result from our thinking solely of our needs and wants rather than the needs of others. Jesus said to love your neighbor as yourself. I suppose there are some people who do not love themselves, but I would classify that as more a mental illness than a sin and even Jesus might accept that. So if we do or do not do anything to or for another human that we would not want done or not done to us, we have sinned.

Now look at Saint Paul's statement and the words corruptible and incorruptible. Our earthly bodies are corrupted because we have sinned, and all of us are guilty. But when we die and leave those corrupted bodies, we go where there is no corruption and no corrupting influences. Why should there be? Our spiritual bodies do not need to be fed or protected from the elements. They will not even need water to avoid dehydration, and they certainly do not need that immense laundry list of unneeded things that might be nice or pleasurable or exciting to have. But when we die, we leave behind these satisfaction-seeking bodies and are left with sin-free bodies, spiritual bodies. And since in heaven there are none of these earthly needs to be satisfied, there is no corruption, just love and companionship in the perfect community of God. And since there also are no health issues from diseases or accidents or even just aging, since we have no earthly bodies to get sick or hurt or age, there's no need for compassion or remorse or sorrow or any other uneasiness of mind. Just love and happiness from and for God. He and our companionship with other spirits will satisfy all our needs. I also feel certain that our spiritual bodies will somehow be fully and individually unique and recognizable so that we won't all just blend into a heavenly cloud of happiness, love, and adoration for eternity. However, that's just another thing we'll have to wait to find out.

That leaves the questions of where and what about hell before we leave our wild speculations about the afterworld. Since we just concluded that sin is completely left behind and our bodies in the spirit world are sinless, regardless of whether we became believers, why is there still a place for hell? Everybody in heaven is pure and perfect regardless of the life he or she led on earth, and if God is going to wait to judge us until we get to the spiritual world as we're told, what's the nature of that judgment and the justification for sending some to hell rather than heaven? Is it because they didn't believe when on earth? Surely that's a sin, but all sins have been forgiven, that is, at least for those who believe. Maybe there is, as the Catholics believe, a purgatory, where the nonbelievers during earthly life remain on parole with a chance to become a believer before ultimately being sent permanently to hell.

If God ultimately judges and punishes for lack of faith here on earth, doesn't this somewhat tarnish His image of being perfectly loving and compassionate? I shudder a bit as I even think that last thought, since it has the sound of blasphemy about it, but I can't somehow avoid thinking that our perfect loving and merciful God carries a bit of vengeance in His nature. The Old Testament God at times certainly admits to such a trait, but don't we believe that God revealed to us His true nature in His Son, Jesus, who never displayed the tiniest suggestion of retribution or vengeance in His life or teachings? However, didn't even Jesus tell us that we would be subject to judgment at the end of time? I'm afraid I'm really getting in over my head, so it's probably best to avoid these kinds of questions, since for each of us they are just the things we won't know until our time comes. As Jesus has told us, now we see dimly, and after death we will see clearly.

Maybe having faith, believing in God, is somewhat like catching a disease. We realize and admit that we are sick with sin and cannot cure ourselves, so we turn our lives over to the ultimate healer, not only for now but also for eternity. If we never realize or admit that we have that disease, we don't need God. We can handle it all ourselves, now and forever. But this is a markedly different disease, one in which the pain and suffering are deferred until much, much later, so how we can be expected to make an educated decision about needing a cure until it's much too late? We feel that we carried out our mortal lives without God's curing help; and after death, we all, believers and unbelievers, are cured anyway; so why then all of a sudden do we now need God? So our eternal life, our hell, would simply be continued, eternal separation from God. Superstring theory certainly allows for more than one nonmaterial world, but hell would be a spiritual world separate from heaven and importantly separate from God. Why not? Superstring theory provides for the possibility of plural worlds, even of similar worlds separate from each other.

I suppose as you advance in years you naturally turn your thoughts more frequently to heaven and what it will be like. It's not so much our arrogant confidence that heaven is where we will be spending eternity as it is, if we believe in a spiritual life after death, where we hope, with God's mercy and patience, we'll fortunately spend eternity with God. After all, our Christian faith tells us that if we believe Jesus is the Son of God, and that He died as a personal offering for the sins of mankind and that if we spend our earthly life following Jesus, we are saved. Of course, there's always that tiny phrase "following Jesus" gnawing at our conscience, but that's too lofty a concern to attempt to rationalize here. The nature of heaven is challenging enough for the moment. So onward and upward.

Unfortunately for me, it's a lot easier to picture what heaven isn't than to visualize what it is. For example, heaven is not material, not made or composed of material stuff, such as this material universe in which we live and in which all that we can now sense or experience. Thus, everything that the Bible tells us about heaven is untrue or, being less dramatic and critical, is symbolic; and that really shouldn't surprise us. The Bible can't describe heaven or the spiritual world or spiritual beings in a way that we will understand, because the necessary vocabulary doesn't exist in human languages. So the Bible does the next best thing. It uses words that we understand as unbelievably desirable, beautiful, pleasurable, and peaceful and leaves it there. So, unfortunately, many of us think of streets of gold, gem-encrusted thrones, etc., as the ambience we will experience when we get to heaven or what we will be denied if we don't. No, there won't be opulent golf courses or fishing holes brimming with ten-pound walleyes or even gorgeous virgins awaiting the Islamic martyrs. I'm sorry, it just cannot be. Heaven—a spiritual world where God, a spiritual being, resides and where we, as the spiritual beings that we will be, are going after the death of our material bodies—will offer nothing material for our edification. It, and everything in it, will be spiritual, whatever that means. There are a few things that we do know. It will be beautiful beyond description, peaceful, disease and pain free, and free of sin; and everything that a spiritual being could need or desire will be supplied gratis. We simply will have to wait to learn what all that amazing last sentence embodies. That's what the Bible tells us in all that symbolic language. You might question, "Where did he get all that information about heaven?" A lot of it came from the Bible.

God's Love Stories

There is a strong feeling that the whole Bible, both the Old Testament and New Testament, is essential to tell God's complete and continuous plan of relationship with humankind. Unfortunately, at times Christian teaching tends to deemphasize the Old Testament as being obsolete and almost irrelevant for true Christian belief. Not so! Neither testament can stand alone. Together, however, their story impacts human faith and commitment in a manner that is synergistic rather than just additive.

"God is love" (1 John 4:8) may be the most startling and thrilling statement in the entire biblical writings. With this, everything else falls into place. Creation is an act of love. The selection of a wandering, landless ethnic group on which to concentrate His initial attention is an act of God's love. God's promise "to be with them" and insisting on a high moral lifestyle in return for God's presence are an act of love, though often it appears to be "tough love"; and finally, God's sacrifice of God's Son for the forgiveness of the Israelites', and humanity's, inherent sinfulness is a supreme act of love. Through God's Son's death and resurrection, the promise of salvation and eternal life to all humankind is love as never before imagined or experienced. The entire Bible is a love story, a story of such incredible importance to us that it is unimaginable that so many can regard it so casually.

Let us start with creation as the Bible does. Our universe and everything in it—and that certainly includes the earth and all of us—do exist; however, the how and why of its creation occupy, for most of us, much less of our thoughts and concerns. Our Christian faith simply states that God did it. But if this were an act of God's love, then ought that not be of much greater importance? Isn't that, even though it only occupies the first two pages of the entire Bible, the beginning of God's long and eventful interaction with humankind?

The remainder of the Old Testament tells of God's dissatisfaction with early humanity's ability or willingness to live according to these standards, of God's selection of Abraham and his offspring as people for God to work closely with, and of the repeated failure of the Jewish people to live their lives according to God's standards. The almost endless sequence of failure, punishment, and ultimate rescue of God's "chosen people" may hardly seem to tell a love story. I suggest it to be a story of God's "tough" love. God appears to be teaching them to their incapability of living sin free lives by their own efforts.

The New Testament, for Christians at least, is much more routinely seen and experienced as the story of Jesus's (God's) love. The aroma of love rises forcefully, pleasurably, from page after page so that it is much easier to recognize this as a love story. The critical thing to remember however is that this is not a new or different story, but it is the fulfillment of the Bible story that started with creation, and the Bible is in its entirety a love story. It is God's plan.

I explained my strong conviction of the importance and significance of both testaments in developing and defining the Christian faith. I am going to present my understanding of the plan God has for His relationship with humanity. I certainly do not presume to have any special knowledge of the workings of God's mind, but rather certain of God's motives that seem to be clearly revealed in the Bible writings, thus allowing some reasonable speculation.

As a Christian, we certainly believe that God created the universe and all its contents. We cannot know why unless God tells us. That, God seems to have neglected to do. God does give us some definite hints. From the very beginning, God reveals an affectionate and pleasurable attitude toward His creation of the "physical world." God saw all that he had made and decided it was very good and blessed it. God also shows a definite friendly and parental attitude toward the first humans. God walks with them in the garden on a daily basis. Now it could be argued that there is nothing special about this period; perhaps God created the universe and then was surprised and was infatuated with these strange creatures on this insignificant planet orbiting this unexceptional star in this "one of a billion" galaxies that God had just made. There is one word in that previous sentence that I object to. Surprise is not a word that can in any way be associated with God. God knows everything, future as well as present and past. Since God is not only omniscient but also omnipotent and internal, everything that has or will happen must be planned. There can be no happenstance.

So I can only assume that God wanted for some reason these beings, these "created in God's image"; their appearance in the creation plan was also integral and maybe even the reason for the whole creation in the first place. The characterization "in his image" is critical. God must have wanted beings with him to share the beauty, comfort, and peace of his spirit world of heaven, who also were thinking beings who knew the difference between good and evil.

When you chewed on this last paragraph for a while and finally swallowed it, all that is left is to spell out the plan that emerges from the essence of the Bible.

THE PLAN

God created the universe to provide the initial home for the beings, to be created in His image. God then desired to share with them through eternity the perfection of heaven. Since their initial home, earth, did not offer the reality of perfection but included the possibility of evil (sin), God initiated a period of trial for failure and forgiveness for these beings. After sufficient training to implant the realization in the minds and souls of these beings of their obvious incomplete capability to attain themselves the necessary perfection to qualify for admission to heaven, God will provide the required sacrifice of Jesus to purify humanity through forgiveness of their inevitable sins and qualify them for admission into heaven. Through His ministry and sacrifice, Jesus establishes God's kingdom on earth to be nurtured and grown by the church in preparation for the ultimate purification of earth from sin and evil in the second coming of Christ.

That is the story that the Bible tells and must have been God's plan. God created our universe and our planet, and there is nothing in God's plan that is not consistent with the description "God is love."

I have now reached that part of God's love story that I expect may offer the greatest challenge to being justified by biblical evidence. So often in the Old Testament, God appears judgmental and even cruel and vindictive rather than loving, and thus to consider the Old Testament to be part of a love story seems questionable. Yet I insist that the Old Testament is an essential part of God's plan and love story.

Following creation, the story continues in Genesis, and for me the first eleven chapters are largely allegorical describing properly mythical events between God and early humanity, which later justify God's establishing moral standards for humanity and choosing a slight group of humans on which to concentrate His attention. Why would God initially select a group of humans on which to shower His attention and love? Again, I cannot read God's mind, but if I wanted an enduring record to be kept—and eventually a written record—it is more likely to happen if I chose a smaller self-contained group of people rather than scatter my attention over all of humanity. God chose Abraham and his progeny, and these are "God's chosen people" of the Old Testament.

Every time we read the Bible, we must remember that all of it was written in ancient times by men to be read by men (and I use the noun men deliberately because in those times women simply were not involved in such activities). That being so, we must then remember that we cannot expect the Bible to contain language that describes naturally occurring events, places, or things in terms consistent with their present knowledge and experience nor spiritual events, places, or things except in language that is pictorial, allegorical.

When reading the Old Testament, unless we kept these previously stated admonitions in the forefront, it is easy to assume all of this to tell of a long and frustrating "learning process" for God. Israelites (humanity) simply are not capable of living lives consistent with God's laws and rules and that some drastically different approaches are necessary to render them qualified for life in heaven. We know by definition that God knows the future and that He knows how the Israelites will react to His prescribed standards. It cannot come as a surprise since God is omniscient. So what is the answer? The Old Testament does tell the story of a learning process and frustratingly repeated cycle of test, failures, punishments, and forgiveness; but the learning is for the Israelites and through them for all of humanity, not for God. God must have deemed it necessary that this humbling fact be pounded into our hard heads repeatedly over centuries. Once we had finally accepted the total impossibility of our qualifying through our own efforts for amendment to eternal life with God, God then could make the supreme sacrifice to atone for our innate sinfulness. Thus, the Old Testament is a long but essential part of God's love story, a period if you will of God's tough love but mandatory if we humans are to understand and accept the crowning act of love as a gift of God that we have not and never can earn through our efforts. If we need further reassurance that the Old Testament contains statements of God's love for us, we find such references in several of its books. In Exodus 34:6–7, when Moses received the two stone tablets from God, these words were used: "compassionate and gracious God, slow to anger abounding in love and faithfulness, maintaining love for thousand generations." This same promise is repeated by God in Numbers 14:18 and Deuteronomy 5:10 beyond this especially in Psalms and among the books of the prophets, innumerable references to God's enduring love for His chosen people. During times of separation in exile, there were plenty of times that the Israelites certainly made bad calls when God's presence was not felt. So love—its presence or seeming absence—prevails throughout the Old Testament.

I describe God's plan for humankind as I understand it or presume it to have been from an interpretation of the Bible's teachings. My assertion is that overall, the Bible describes God's loving interaction with humankind. The plan assumes that God's desire for humans may have provided the essential impetus for the creation itself. That sounds a bit arrogant—in fact a whole lot of are—but it is hard to explain God's reason for creating our universe in any other way. God's involvement in the universe since creating it is confined to God's interaction with the first humans here on earth. If you reject that statement, then all that is left is that God created the universe out of sheer boredom and has ignored it ever since. If so, the fact that we are here is just a happenstance, nothing more.

My faith tells me that with God, we count. In fact, God's whole direction with humankind is a story of God's love for us. Therefore, first God had to create us. That takes only the first two pages of the Bible to describe. However, if this were to be a sound and growing love affair, the affection between God and humanity must flow in both directions, and that has been the never-ending problem with which God has contended. But that is dealt with in a remainder of the Bible and will be discussed in greater detail there.

Back to creation. The first and most important thing disclosed in the Bible account of creation is as follows: "God created humankind in his image, in the image of God he created them; male and female he created them" (Genesis 1:27 NRSV). In what unique way does humankind differ from all other living things? Humans think and reason and know the difference between right and wrong even though they at times have trouble on the boundaries of those perimeters. Humans thus are godlike in their mental and moral makeup. Is it so hard to believe that God wanted beings closely akin to Himself to associate with in His eternal existence and that He would love them? It might be harder to understand why God continued to love them after centuries of failures on their part and disappointment and frustration. For God, of course, that was no surprise to Him and His plan. The only other suggestion of God's love for mankind that I have found in the creation story itself is in the second description of creation (Genesis 2:18), it is not good to be alone. Without female companionship and a partner in reproduction, the man could not fully realize his humanity.

Lastly, even though the entire description of creation in the Bible takes up only a little more than one and a half pages, its importance in the story of God's love affair with humankind is primal and critical. In fact, creation tells us the reason the remainder of the Bible story has been written because God first loved humankind!

Now we come to that part of the Bible that is all about God showering His unconditional love on humanity. The New Testament starts with the four gospels, each of which tells the story of Jesus Christ's ministry here on earth. Jesus is Son of God. So what we read here is a description of God—God in human form through His Son, Jesus, so that He is perfectly understandable by all other humans. If there is one thing obvious about Jesus, it is His love. The Apostle John says it clearly and bluntly, "God is love" (1 John 4:8). This is not love as humans experience it. This is love of a dimension and character beyond our imagination. This is God all-powerful, all-knowing, and eternal voluntarily sacrificing Himself, suffering excruciating pain and ultimately death as a sacrifice for the sins of all humanity, a humanity that is completely unworthy of such a sacrifice. This is love beyond measure and beyond our ability to understand. All that God asks in return is that we believe and turn our lives to Him. God knows that even though we comply, we will still sin again, but that too will be forgiven, and He still loves us forever. What more needs to be said? There is a great deal more to say about love in the New Testament. Jesus sacrificing to secure our salvation is fundamental to our faith. Jesus's entire ministry here on earth is a love story that He demonstrates in His healing particularly of the unfortunate and the attention He lavishes is on the outcast and disadvantaged. He makes God's loving nature particularly evident in His actions and in His teachings and parables. God seems immediately transformed from a distant and judgmental parent into a concerned and affectionate father. If we miss this revelation in the New Testament, we miss a good bit of its essential message.

However, God's love story does not end here. All you have to do is turn on your TV to the news or read the morning paper to face graphic evidence that life here on earth has not come close to God's expectations for His kingdom. There are some Christians who believe that the transformation to His kingdom must wait for Christ to come again, and if you examine the improvement in human condition in the past two thousand years or so, you will agree that though there has been some improvement over this span of time, we still have a long, long way to go. Slavery may have largely been eliminated in the world, but covert subjugation remains and often with even more heinous implications. So we can hardly claim that God's kingdom has been established here on earth, or can we? Was it in fact one of the specific purposes of sending Jesus to earth as a human was to do justice, to establish God's kingdom, and to start the church of all believers in order to develop, grow, and strengthen that kingdom? Isn't that part of God's plan? And that kind of drops the ball right in our laps. If we do not see much progress in human morality in the past two millennia, whose fault is it? I'm not suggesting that there will not be a second coming of Christ; the Bible clearly foretells us, and we'll discuss that at another time. What seems obvious to me is that God has already given us a job to do, each one of us, and how long it takes before God's kingdom here reaches a state of development necessary to justify the second coming is in human hands with God's description and help of course, and we better get about it. Maybe we need to talk to God privately about this. Is not it reasonable to turn to the source of such knowledge and power if we hold for any chance of success?

Nuff said!

Tidbits to Ponder

CHILDREN OF GOD

Some time ago, I came across a five-minute video by Leonce Crump, pastor of Renovation Church in Atlanta, that dealt in a very moving and basic Christian matter with the cultural conflict that we experience here in America and throughout the world. Pastor Crump described his church as being transcultural rather than multicultural, one in which the members were first children of God and secondarily White or African American or whatever their background was. He likened it to a tapestry in which the individual images were woven together into a magnificent and meaningful composite while each individual picture retained its own original beauty. I was strongly moved by this way of looking at life and struck by how many of the problems we face today would be solved if we approached social or political questions in this manner. In our federal and state governments, why must every issue be dealt with as Republican versus Democrat rather than assessing the relevant social and moral factors before reach a decision?

I am afraid I am being too simplistic. The tapestry analogy applies beautifully to a church or congregation, where all the members at the outset have Christian faith in common. Such is not so in a community or country.

Even in America, a strong wall has been erected in the Constitution between religion and government. However, a great majority of our politicians profess to some religious commitment, I expect mostly Christian. Some, I suppose, only do so to get elected; but regardless, we must have in all of our legislatives a good number of committed Christians. Why don't they act like it? The fact that reality often rears its ugly head whenever I get excited by one of my idealistic trains of thought doesn't stop me from wishing and hoping. If we believe that God's kingdom is already at work here on earth and the kingdom's growth and strengthening is our task as followers of Christ, *we'd better get busy*!

THE FIRST MIRACLE

On Easter Sunday in 2019, I was introduced to a new analogy, one that I had never heard before in an Easter sermon. The analogy spoke of the unquestioning acceptance of the miracle of new life that occurs every time a fetus is created in a mother's womb as compared to the almost universal questioning and lack of acceptance of the miraculous creation of new spiritual life at the death of a human. Of course, the understandable difference is that the first of these events for each of us is in the past, while the second is necessarily in the future. Despite the fact that we as individual beings have zero memory of that first miracle in our human lives, or of the nine months we spent in the womb, or of the first few months out in the "real world," we still have no problem accepting it as fact because we know it did happen regardless of whether we understand any or all of it. And the miracle that results in the creation of new human life is just as marvelous and as awe-inspiring as the miracle transformation of human to spiritual life that occurs after death, except that it is in the unknown future. Even though we've been told by God that it will happen, we still have difficulty accepting the fact as truth.

IMAGINE WITH ME

One of the most serious barriers to the successful teaching of the Christian faith to eager neophytes is the insistence of overzealous authorities that the Bible be accepted as the unerring and literal word of God, that it must be accepted without question or explanation as true word for word. Thus, contrary to current knowledge or even to the implications of simple reason, the world was created by God. In six days, the first woman was created by God by taking a rib from the first man. Noah built a boat and loaded two of every kind of living thing into it and sailed around for forty days while the entire surface was covered with a cleansing layer of water, to mention just a few of the more difficult truths imposed by biblical literalists. If, to believe, you must believe without question such "mythical teachings," then it may become equally impossible to believe other and more fundamental teachings of the Bible. In fact, the underpinnings of the Christian faith may be rejected. Why is it so essential that we accept fanciful language as literal truth when it's obvious that God, through His prophets and raconteurs, was obliged to use language that could be understood by them and their readers, millennia ago, language that today seems at least fanciful, if not ridiculous?

Imagine with me. You find yourself on an isolated island in the vastness of an endless ocean. The only native inhabitants are a tribe of very primitive people, who never in the history of their existence have had any contact the outside world. They are friendly, and they take you in and provide for your needs. They have a function, but very simple language, which in time you learn sufficiently to communicate with them. However, they have a polytheistic religion, which probably understandably idolizes the natural force that from time to time present them with life-threatening crisis. Alarmingly, when the threat is sufficiently severe, their religious practices may turn to human sacrifices to appease their gods. So you feel pressed to somehow explain to them that the sun, wind, fire, etc., which they worship out of fear, are not responsive to their ritualistic efforts, but the God they should be worshiping is an all-powerful, all-knowing spiritual God who created all that they see, feel, and know. How would you go about explaining this in a manner that had meaning to them yet did not depend upon all that we have learned scientifically and socially that would be totally incomprehensible to them? You might well create a story for them that sounded very much like the book of Genesis.

WHO? ME?

Anyone who reads the Bible or even just listens in church to readings from the gospels is familiar with statements that Jesus made regarding our obligations if we are to inherit eternal life.

"Sell everything you have and give to the poor and you will have treasure in heaven. Then come, follow me" (Luke 18: 22).

"And everyone who has left houses and brothers or sisters or father or mother or children or fields for my sake will receive a hundred times as much and will inherit eternal life" (Matthew 19:29).

My silent but nevertheless response to such pronouncements is, "Who? Me?" We can't believe that God is really asking or expecting us to give up everything associated with a normal life and spend our earthly existence serving the poor, serving others. I've worked so hard to get where I am. My family needs me. I can't believe that God really means that. What would happen to the world, to the world's economy, to our government, and to our school systems if everyone did that? Love your neighbor as yourself is a goal, but is it possible in this life? Unreasonable demands? God (Jesus) gives us the overall objective, the long range, the eternal goal. You shall be perfect as God is perfect. Paul gives us the reality that in this life we are all sinners no matter how hard we try, and we are saved only through the *grace of God.*

Part 2

Science and Religion

A common and long-standing premise in the ongoing controversy that supposedly exists between science and religion is that it's not possible for a seriously dedicated scientist to commit honestly to a belief in God. Such arguments are founded on the basic "fact" that there is no scientific evidence that any "world" exists other than the natural three-dimensional material world in which we live. Since supernatural phenomena and supernatural beings cannot exist in this world, it should be obvious that they cannot exist at all and, thus, no god or miracles!

After retirement, several things happened in my life. I now had the time to devote some serious study to getting to know God better. I relocated to Arizona, remarried, and my wife seemed to have such a close personal relationship with God. I wanted that too! I met a new friend who seemed to have rejected his faith in God and actually challenged my belief! Scary. So I decided to search for some answers. To my surprise, I have found two compelling answers, both major and well-accepted scientific theories that have emerged in the past century, since the time when I was acquiring my scientific training. These have solidified—I could say cemented—my faith. In an authentic way, science, the expected foe of religion, has instead provided me with strong and significant commitment to my belief in God.

The first of these scientific proposals from the field of cosmology is the big bang theory, which describes the process by which our universe was created at a specific time and place in the past. The place—a spot in space—is not significant for our present argument; but the time, some 13.7 billion years ago, is significant. The essence of the theory was first proposed in 1927 by a Belgian Catholic priest/scientist named Lemaitre. It suggests that at some point in time all the mass and energy in our universe was contained in an infinitely small particle under infinite pressure, called a singularity, and that the compressing force was instantaneously removed and the particle allowed to expand, not explode, and continue that expansion to the present. This theory clearly states that our universe was created, and if created, there must be a cause or creator.

In the middle 1900s, there was a competing proposal called the steady state theory, but as the science of cosmology advanced, the big bang theory has emerged as most widely accepted by the scientific community. Why is this critical in our quest for an answer? There were those opponents of belief in God who suggested that rather than a specific starting point, our universe had just always existed, expanding, and contracting throughout eternity. But the big bang theory demands that there be a singularity, a starting entity. There are sound reasons in the fields of cosmology and subatomic physics for this requirement that are beyond my ken, but there is one very compelling reason that I could understand. With the scientific advances of the past seventy-five years, it has been possible to determine with considerable accuracy that the present universe is expanding along precise pathways and at a measurable rate. When such pathways are extrapolated back in time, they converge to a single point at roughly 13.7 billion years ago. It was at that time and point in space that the creation of our universe took place.

Since there is no possibility of the formation by natural causes of such an entity as the required singularity and the "it's just always been there" proposal is rejected, the big bang creation remains as the only reasonable cause. "Reasonable?" you question. Well, if we can find no natural cause, then we must look for a cause that is supernatural. Why not God? Can you think of another?

We do get help in finding a solution to this knotty problem, and surprisingly, it too comes from science. Until the nineteenth century, classic physics felt that it fully understood the laws and workings of the material world in which we live. Since then, and with considerable acceleration in the twentieth century, new findings and explanations (theories) have shaken that confidence with the confirmation and widespread acceptance of Einstein's theories of "special" and "general" relativity and the mass of discoveries in subatomic physics, which have led to the solidification of fact and theory in quantum physics from science to justify our belief in a supernatural being as our creator. Both relativity and quantum physics are now firmly established in their places in modern physics. Each has formulated solid mathematical descriptions of its essence. However, if each is to be accepted as essential to an understanding of our universe, their separate mathematics must be compatible.

They aren't! That has been a compelling problem for the past twenty years or so, sufficiently compelling that many of the top scientists in the field have addressed it. Almost unbelievably in such short time, a new theory of the fundamental nature of the material world has been proposed, "string theory," and modified, "superstring theory," with the surprising requirement that the universe not be restricted to the four dimensions (three spatial and time) stipulated by relativity, but eleven dimensions, including our four, in order for the mathematics of superstring theory to be compatible with the mathematics of both relativity and quantum physics. This is a very new theory but is highly regarded, and though experimental evidence is required to confirm and refine it—and it has a bit of a science fiction aura about it—it is widely accepted as worthy with expectations and hype.

Why is this important in justifying our Christian belief? Remember, classic physics demanded that our existence and our thinking be restricted to our known natural three-dimensional world, and thus no supernatural beings or events allowed and so no God. But now, we've eleven dimensions to deal with, and even though science doesn't tell us at this point what those extra dimensions may provide, they at least don't exclude the possibility of God and heaven. Now, science and religion might even be considered as allies. How about that!

Something called the superstring theory provides for the possibility of plural worlds, even of similar worlds separate from each other. As I reach this point in my study of what science has newly added to our understanding of God's creation, I suddenly realize that they have really given us very little to help us understand or explain our religious beliefs. Rather, science has merely given us some assurance that we are not idiots to believe in and dream of an afterlife with God, whereas previously science had told us that what we believed was impossible. Basically, we're left with our faith, but with our faith strengthened.

For me, when considering God's involvement in the creation of our world—of the universe and everything in it as we know it—it's a compelling start to accept that our world was created, that it hasn't just always been here. The big bang theory, the current most commonly accepted theory on the formation of the universe, is based on the scientific observation that the universe is expanding at a measurable rate. Extrapolating this expansion back in time produces paths that intersect in space at a point and at a time some fourteen plus billion years ago. This, to me, suggests that science itself has provided the justification for a supernatural creator for our universe; for, if as the big bang theory suggests that at some long-ago spot in space and time all of the material substance of our universe was accumulated together at one point, there clearly must have been someone or something to act as a cause for this event. The theory goes on to call this spot, this entity, a "singularity," which consisted of all the matter in the universe compacted under infinite pressure into an infinitesimally small space.

I can hear you say, "Get serious! That's impossible!" But a lot of eminent physicists and cosmologists accept the theory as reasonable and will continue to test and argue the point. Whether with the passage of time the big bang theory is proven with certainty, modified, or replaced with some more scientifically accepted theory is unimportant for me. The creation of our world by some force predating and outside of itself is now established as a fact, and we can proceed to assign some cause as having produced that event. One reasonable course is to call that force God. So far, in my estimation, there has been no plausible competing suggestion.

As an example of such competition, I just read on the Internet a printed 2005 lecture by Stephen Hawking titled "the Origin of the Universe" in which Hawking, a renowned and highly respected physicist and mathematician, strongly supports the big bang theory, but emphatically rejects God as even existing, let alone playing any part in the creation of the universe. In 2012, Hawking coauthored with Leonard Mlodinow the book *the Grand Design* in which the authors suggest that because of gravity "the universe can and will create itself from nothing" and "spontaneous creation is the reason there is something rather than nothing, why the universe exists, why we exist." In other words, gravity is the designer and creator of the universe. This rather surprising and strange-sounding suggestion purports to be based on the latest in quantum physics involving string theory and even beyond that M-theory, which postulates eleven dimensions rather than just the four found in our space-time universe. I need not bother admitting that such speculation goes far beyond my education and present knowledge in physics, so let's just back off for a moment and consider their position based on nothing more than good old "horse sense." They suggest that gravity created our universe from nothing. But isn't gravity something? My physics taught me that gravity is the attracting force that acts between two material objects, so if no material entities, nothing, existed before creation, how could gravity? Is that a tough question?

So I turned to Wikipedia, hoping to find there in the discussion of Hawking and Mlodinow's book comments pro and con by knowledgeable contributors. There are many lengthy plaudits, mostly by avant-garde atheistic physicists, but even more lengthy criticisms by both physicists and theologians. The scientific negatives mostly suggest that the authors have reached their conclusion by relying on lofty, untested, and in some instances unsound extensions of accepted science. Among the most reasonable of these were suggestions that the authors should limit themselves to presenting their theory to the scientific community for discussion and testing, rather than dwelling at such length on its theological implications. Should their theory gain wide acceptance by science, theology will have to take note.

One of the most awkward and infuriating aspects of theorizing in this supernatural or "spiritual" realm is that everything we know, everything we can talk about or measure, is limited to things of this world. We can't talk or theorize about any aspect of the "spirit world" or, to put it in scientific language, about any details of worlds having dimensions other than our four space-time dimensions except by using the wildest speculations. Why, because things of this world are the entirety of the things that we can sense, personally, or even with our most advanced scientific instruments. Yet God, by definition, is not of this world, which makes it impossible for us to prove that God even exists, let alone that God created our universe, or even to speculate descriptively on how that might have come about. Using the same logic, nor are we able to say that

God does not exist! So does that leave us with no alternative other than meekly to say, "It's a matter of faith"? I'm afraid so, except that our faith is strongly fortified by good supportive evidence. So, although it's certainly true that we cannot prove scientifically that God created the universe, or even that God exists, there are strong and reasonable reasons to accept both of these beliefs on faith.

As I stated at the outset, the most compelling "proof" for me is found in our universe itself. Conclusions drawn from scientifically valid observations and measurements of our present-day cosmos strongly point to the fact that our universe had a point and time of origin. What, then, existed before this point in time? As far as we know, nothing, at least nothing of our space-time material universe. This means that, since nothing existed before but now our universe exists, there must be a reason—it didn't just happen. This enormous quantity of "stuff" that makes up all the billions of stars and their planets and comets and meteors that comprise the universe had to come from somewhere. It had to be created. Even when we ascribe the creation to God, we have to provide some explanation, and this is where it really gets good.

We can't, but we must have one, so the answer must be something that we know nothing about, something that we cannot see, touch, or experience in any way, except through the realization that it must be there. It must exist. Also, it must have powers and intelligence far beyond anything that we through our experience can understand or explain. Thus, our awareness of God arises not because of our creative ability but because God is inevitable and must already possess these capabilities in order to explain our existence.

So an all-powerful, all-knowing, infinite being has to exist outside of and before this space-time universe in which we live. Why not God?

Since humankind has existed, there have been those of us who have rejected this "truth." Some claim that our universe has always been here, that the universe itself is infinite in time and space. With our advancing technology, however, we have shown that to be untrue. Recently, some like Hawking have chosen to negate the logical laws of cause and effect and to offer the theory that it's quite reasonable that the universe could have been created from nothing by nobody and that this incredibly enormous and unthinkably complex production could just happen of its own volition. They base this on an area of advanced thinking called quantum physics, which reaches into dimensions other than those of our known world and at advanced stages can become truly speculative. There is nothing new or abhorrent about the suggestion that there are other dimensions and other worlds than ours. Such ideas have been common in both science fiction and in serious scientific theorizing. Also, if God exists, God has to live in some other world than ours, a world that existed before ours. So, in a very real sense, our understanding of God is not at all inconsistent with our scientific and logical experience.

However, on what basis then do we ascribe to God certain characteristics and personality? Is there substantial evidence that God is loving and that God had some particular motivation in creating the material world? We all, in spite of our religious background and training, are at least aware of the Bible. That book contains the essence of our Christian faith and in the Old Testament, which the

Jews call the Torah, of the Jewish faith. Clearly none of it was directly written by God, but by humans who were strongly moved by their interaction with God to provide a lasting record of their thoughts and experiences relating to God. All of the Old Testament was first written more than two millennia ago, most of it much earlier than that, and for none of it is the original manuscript available or is the author positively known. Much of the early Old Testament writings undoubtedly existed first as oral tradition and are couched in picturesque language so as to be meaningful to primitive humans. Even so, much of the geographic and historic events and places in this early material has since been authenticated by archeological and historical research.

A compelling reason for accepting the Bible writings as God's word is that for centuries being a known believer meant suffering discrimination, injustice, and even cruel and terrifying persecution. Yet the Jews willingly underwent such suffering as certainly did the earlier Christians. For what reason? If there was a reward, it was not visible to reasonable thinking people. Add to those two factors for both faiths, that for centuries from a handful of committed adherents, against unimaginable adversities including attempted annihilation, both religions have survived and now are vigorous.

One final factor relating to our beliefs and faith is that many of the arguments against God and actions ascribed to God, and certainly this applies to miracles, are that such negative thinking as, "That's not possible. Gravity acts on all material objects. Walk on water, ridiculous! If you're dead, you're dead." I agree that it's not possible for such actions to be performed by mere humans under the natural laws of this world—except God is not of this world. Remember who God is. God is omnipotent and omniscient. Can we tell God what He can and cannot do? If God could make this world, couldn't He decide what things He can do here. So I conclude that the proof of God's existence and nature is plentifully supplied for our faith.

But there is one last question that cries out for an answer. If God created our universe, why? Just for us? Can we be so arrogant as to suggest that the all-knowing and all-powerful God went to the trouble of producing all of this enormous, extravagant, and unbelievably complex universe, billions and billions of stars, each with numbers of orbiting planets and moons and unnumbered comets, meteors, and asteroids sailing about in between, just so He could have us? Well, maybe not just so, but at least so that God could have us among other consequences of the creation that we know nothing about, but that may very well be there or will be or were. It would be the ultimate presumption to suggest that we could read God's mind or deduce His intentions. But God did tell us some things. In His message to us, the Bible, in the very first chapter, God made it clear that He did not only create our universe and it all was good, but that He created humans on earth in His image. It is clear that we, in our earthly form, do not look like God. We are material beings, designed to operate in a physical world and subject to aging and deterioration; but God is a spirit, not of this world, and infinite. The usual definition of image refers to a visual impression, but even our language offers the possible definition of "semblance or likeness," which can refer to our personality, character, or intellect rather than physical appearance. So God created us in His likeness as thinking beings with a conscience, knowing good from bad, and with a will allowed to choose between the two. We are also told that God created us to be His companions, that He shared time with us, walked with us on earth until our disobedience forced Him to terminate that pleasure. God's first command upon our actions was that we should love Him, respect and honor, and obey Him. Throughout the Old Testament, and certainly through His sending His Son to atone for our disobedience and thus qualify us, He has made clear that it is His strong desire to have us with Him in His world through eternity. Are we then presumptuous to assume that at least one of God's reasons for the creation of the universe was to provide Him with us? No, this then allows us to conclude humbly and thankfully that all this was not just a spur-of-the-moment reaction to boredom by God but rather a planned action with a purpose and that at least part of that purpose was our creation and rearing and ultimate qualification as His eternal companions in His heavenly kingdom.

The New Physics of Christian Faith

I've used the term "new physics" as distinct from classic Newtonian physics to embrace all that quantum and sub-atomic physics and cosmology have provided in the past 150 years toward our understanding of the nature and makeup of our universe and the material world in which we live. This centers around Einstein's relativity theories, the big bang theory, and superstring and M-theories. I don't think I have to dwell lengthily on my profound awareness of my lack of ability to understand or discuss the details of any of this science, but fortunately, there are people who have interpreted these discoveries and postulations into descriptions that are understandable and meaningful to laypeople. I'm just hoping that these guys have got it right.

As a start, I want to mention these sources, as follows: *the Elegant Universe* (1999), *the Fabric of the Cosmos* (2004), and *the Hidden Reality* (2011) by Brian Greene and *Quantum Christianity* (2011) by Jim Groves and *Quantum Mechanics* (2012) by Eliot Hawkins.

In *the Fabric of the Cosmos*, Brian Greene gets into superstring theory and the introduction of the recent theoretical entity called a brane. While a string is a tiny one-dimensional bit of energy, a brane is a two- or more dimensional entity that exist in conjunction with strings that make up the matter and forces existent in the subatomic world. Einstein established that we live in a four-dimensional universe, three spatial dimensions and time. The smallest brane would be a two-brane that would be a membrane not a string; thus from "membrane" comes the name "brane." These string and brane concepts are compatible with the mathematics of the associated theories.

New experimental findings lead to a reworking of the mathematics and the suggestion of new possibilities. One of the most astonishing results of all this flurry of activity in quantum physics and cosmology has been that the mathematics of string and M-theory now require additional dimensions over the four of Einstein. The latest theory to emerge, called M-theory, is defined by mathematics that require eleven dimensions, ten spatial dimensions and time, which has led to the concept of "brane worlds" containing multiple branes of varying dimensions ranging from three-spatial to ten-spatial, called 3-branes and 10-branes, respectively. And finally comes the ultimate speculation that our universe, this material world in which we live, is actually a 3-brane located in a brane world that may very well have any number of accompanying branes of various dimensions. So suddenly, we religious thinkers, who have for centuries been continuously put on the defensive by science for even suggesting that there is another world, a supernatural world called heaven in which resides a supernatural being called God, find ourselves thrust by that same science into the realm of a brane world in which multiple, even an infinite number of, other universes coexist, universes like ours or of such wildly speculative composition as to make our hair stand on end. Now, this is still all theory, but theory that has been supported and advanced by experimental findings and has received wide acceptance by the serious scientific community.

I was just digging myself out from under this enigmatic pile when I happened on Brian Greene's most recent book *the Hidden Reality* and felt the blast of an even larger bomb. Greene has written this new book not only to extend his discussion of brane world universes but also to describe at least a half-dozen other theories that have been proposed and that also postulate multiple universes. These new proposals are described in separate chapters, subtitled "the Quilted Multiverse," "the Inflationary Multiverse," "the Landscape Multiverse," "the Quantum Multiverse," and "the Holographic Multiverse" as well as "the Brane and Cyclic Multiverses." I had just begun gleefully to attack the mysteries of the brane world and to speculate on how and where God might fit into that picture when I'm broadsided by a barrage of additional multiverse possibilities. And science had the temerity to suggest that religion had overstepped the bounds of reason! How could I possibly figure out where God could or would fit in this confused picture? The conclusion I've reached is that I no longer have to feel compelled to defend my belief in supernatural events, places, and beings and now can focus my thoughts and activities on advancing God's kingdom here on earth. When science begins to make some sense out of this confusing mélange it has created will be time enough to tackle that other problem. I recently have become aware of a rather strange sequence of religious experiences in which I have been involved. The strangeness is due to the fact that I have become involved in these events arbitrarily, but there appears to be a definite commonality between the individual experiences as if my exposed to them resulted from adherence to a plan. Whose plan? Definitely not mine!

To explain, all three events involved books that I have read, all by different authors. The first was rather gentle but still provocative; the second enlightening, stirring, and largely satisfying; the third gripping and revolutionary, if applicable. Last fall, I learned of a discussion group at my local church, which was to read and discuss over a number of weeks the book *How God Became King* by N. T. Wright. Wright's thesis is that the organized church has over the centuries neglected one of the most important messages of the four canonic gospels in their statements of faith, teachings, and preaching. They have strongly emphasized the atonement and salvation procured for us through Christ's crucifixion, resurrection, and ascension but have failed to recognize that Christ, through his life and ministry, also initiated God's kingdom here on earth at that time. The impact being that today and over the past two thousand years, we, the believers and members of the church, are engaged in building and refining God's kingdom on earth, rather than waiting for the "end of time" for His kingdom to come. Such a belief could and should have a significant effect on how we live our lives.

At Christmas, my grandson gave me a trilogy written by Brian D. McLaren titled *A New Kind of Christianity, the Story We Find Ourselves In*, and *the Last Word and the Word After That*. Throughout these three books, the author tells a fictional story that details a nontraditional way of interpreting the Bible and the implications that this new thinking has on how we live our lines. The story is of a pastor, Dan, who, in midlife, begins to develop some serious questions about his "fundamentalist" faith and is even thinking of abandoning the pastoral vocation. He meets and becomes a close friend of an ex-pastor, Neil, who has recanted and become a high school science teacher and who leads Dan in what Neil calls "postmodern" thinking about the Bible and Christian living and practice. He treats the Bible, from end to end, as a story—the story—of God's interaction with humanity, in a way that I found interesting, very much in line with some of my own ideas and definitely at odds with fundamentalist Bible interpretation. The language of the Bible is accepted literally only to the extent that it is historical. A lot of attention is given in the third book of the trilogy to questions of heaven and hell, to the nature of God's judgment and our salvation. Neil presents creation as a continuing process, consistent with modern science but not offensive to religious belief. Even evolution can fit into the picture without stress. McLaren doesn't propose a new church, just updated and revised language and thinking, but there are many who will have to make adjustments if this is to be accepted.

A week ago, a friend—not through church connections since he is Baptist and I an Episcopalian turned Lutheran, but through profession since we are both retired scientists, a friend with whom I have had numerous religious discussions—gave me a book titled *Proof of Heaven* by Eben Alexander. This is a description by a respected neurosurgeon and neurological scientist of a near-death experience that he lived through and from which he recovered completely. The description is gripping. The interpretation would dramatically and drastically alter our faith regarding heaven and hell, earthly and afterlife, and the nature of the "universe" and relation of the earth to it. It's a short book, only 171 pages, but I found it so compelling that I nearly read it nonstop. Again, if I find I can completely accept the description of the "unknowable" that Alexander presents, then it will have added substantial meat to the bones of some thoughts that I have had and some very challenging life-living directions for me. The big question is, "What to do about it, if anything?" It's interesting that both McLaren and Alexander have done something concrete. Brian McLaren is a founding member of www.emergentvillage. com and a blog, Emergent Village Voice. The members, called Friends, make the following four commitments:

1. To God in the Way of Jesus
2. To the church in all of its forms
3. To God's world
4. To one another

And then they further the movement both personally and congregationally. Dr. Alexander is cofounder of Eternea, a nonprofit charity whose mission is to advance research, education, and applied programs concerning spiritually transformative experiences, which is represented by www.eternea.org. I don't know how successful or active either of these organizations is. Eternea appears more aimed at gathering information concerning the relationship of the spiritual and material worlds, while Emergent Village seems to have a closer religious tie-in.

The book *Quantum Christianity* by Jim Groves is not written by a scientist, but rather by an ex-Presbyterian minister who has become a technical writer for Microsoft. I've included this reference because it suggests another person's thoughts on how the "new physics" relates to Christian faith and belief. With that brief introduction, I'm going to plunge right into my major subject. As you can see, Brian Greene is a major source of scientific interpretation of new physics, as I've titled it. He is a noted and well-regarded theoretical physicist, Columbia University professor, and author. I have no idea what his religious beliefs are. It doesn't matter. I have never suggested that science now has proved the existence of God, but that science has now opened the door to allow rather than deny speculation regarding other worlds than this material world in which we live. Having said that, I've included a letter from a dear friend who is a physicist.

Bill,

I read the book Quantum Christianity by Jim Groves as you recommended. You made a few comments to me about the physics involved. From my understanding, I think he has that right from a number of perspectives. His recitation of the work of Newton and its deterministic core is right. The philosophical extrapolation to all of nature certainly has been a core belief of those whose philosophy and, for that matter, religion is science. I like his analysis of the essence of "science" in that it is deterministic—effects have causes— and so given complete knowledge of the initial conditions, the results can be calculated mathematically. Another matter is that of all you sense is all of what you have, that is, all that exists. If it is not observable, it does not exist. A corollary is that if it is not repeatable, it is not. Perhaps the greatest contribution of Newton is that he firmly tied physical reality to mathematics. It is not really obvious that if you describe something with a mathematical equation, and then ignore the physical system and pursue mathematics wherever it takes you, when you are done, and assuming no dropped signs, the final mathematical expressions also describe physical reality. When that has been doubted, the math wins out and new aspects of reality are discovered. One example is that when expressions were developed for the charge on an electron, the final equation was in terms of the charge squared. If the square root is taken, both positive charges and negative charges are possible. Obviously, electrons are negative. But further investigation led to the discovery of positively charged electrons, now called positrons. Positrons are "antimatter" of electrons. When they join, they annihilate leaving two photons without mass or charge, pure energy, traveling in opposite directions. Positron emission tomography, or PET scans, is a practical medical application.

The success of mathematics is what drives modern physics and cosmology. I liked Groves' explanation of general relativity. It came about after I stopped taking coursework and my field was much more mundane. I measured temperature for most of my professional life. I also liked his recognition that the practitioners of secular science philosophy or religion are as narrow minded as the fundamentalist Christians he disparages. He expresses, too, the wave-particle dilemma quite well along with the fundamental Heisenberg Uncertainty Principle. Our knowledge is limited to a certain irreducible uncertainty that is absolutely fundamental, not just a technological limitation.

Finally, I liked his discussion of the need-to-know God and his analogy to knowing his wife. It certainly was a beautiful expression of what a good marriage is, if only partially or occasionally attainable. I guess that is true of our relationship to God, also only partially and occasionally attainable. Nevertheless, I think he characterizes the confrontation between science and religion too starkly. While there are extremist and blind adherents on both sides, I know and know of many scientists who are devout Christians. They are also serious thinkers. The history of wins for the scientific method is not one sided nor are the debates as simple-minded as the science historians characterize them. Both the Galileo affair and the evolution debate are far more complex and subtle than commonly taught.

Science is great at what it does and with what it deals. But revelation is not to be disparaged. It has served pretty well in describing the human condition for at least as long as the Bible relates it. Modern sociological studies, after much social debate, come around to suggest that kids do better with both parents and family unity helps. People do not much like "just getting along", we would rather fight. The Ten Commandments would not have been given if stealing, etc. We're not a problem. I have not yet seen or read of any convincing discussion of the development of a moral conscience. That came when man was created in the image of God.

I do not agree with Groves' theology of the nature of God. I have heard others express that all mind is united as one in some multidimensional universe sense, but it makes God part or integral with His creation. That He participates in it is reasonable, but as you noted in your letter a while back, if it was made, it required a Maker. Groves does not give full credence to the Holy Scriptures as being from God. For him, they are the impressions of thoughtful men over the ages. That is commonly taught, I believe, in what we fundamentalists disparage as "liberal" seminaries.

My own synthesis of modern physics (quantum theory and relativity) is that first there is plenty we do not know and, indeed, cannot know. Multi-dimensional reality leaves lots of room for God and a spirit world that is insensible to us. We are limited creatures. The uncertainty principle allows for the paradox of free will and divine providence, even as wave-particle duality cannot be denied. The fact that the physics of the experienced world (Newton) is insufficient for the very large or very small suggests that the observable Darwinian evolution of species and traits within themselves—as in vaccine research, or bird beaks—may not be adequate to explain the origin of life, the presence of different kinds, such as cats and dogs or humans. I am not a naturalist. Certainly, random mutation and survivability is not tenable biological science or statistically probable. Unfortunately, or maybe fortunately, origins science, both physical and biological, is not repeatable.

These are a few of my thoughts. I no longer fear that science will disprove my religion and I have grown to accept that "now we see through a glass darkly, then we shall see face to face. Then shall I know, even as I am known,"

Thanks for the stimulating reads, both Groves' book and your statement of faith.

TOM

Why Believe in God

Right from the outset, there are a couple of things that we need to get straight in order to tackle this question. First of all, if you're requiring scientific proof that God exists, forget it. There isn't any and, very well, never will be. That said, the second thing is that neither is there scientific proof that God doesn't exist nor will there probably ever be.

That leaves us with three options. Since there is no proof that God exists, we can choose to believe that He doesn't, or since there's no proof that He doesn't exist, we can choose to believe that He does, or since there's no proof either way, we can choose to examine the data further to see if there's any good reason to lean one way or the other. That's what I have done personally and what I plan to discuss from this point on.

Not surprisingly, there is not much scientific evidence in support of the existence of God; as a matter of fact, you could probably say none. As I said, why would you expect there to be? Science deals with and is limited to things and aspects of the material world in which we live. Since the God that we worship is not a material being—He is spirit—our science has no basis for being able to detect God or in any way measure Him. So much for scientific proof of God. But there is another form of proof called logical proof, not quite as absolute as scientific, though still acceptable as an alternative. In proving something logically, you examine all the known evidence, and if logic tells you that this evidence compels a certain conclusion, there is a high likelihood that it is true.

Let me give you an example. As Galileo stood at the top of the Tower of Pisa, he knew from experience and observation that a ball released from his hand would fall to the ground and that if he were to step off the tower, he would also fall and be smashed on the pavement below. Using this logically attained "fact," he carefully avoided any misstep as he descended the tower. Science knew very little about gravity in Galileo's day, probably not even its name, except about certain of its effects; and those were compelling enough for him logically to act in a definite manner. Isn't it interesting that even though we've learned a bit more about this fascinating force called gravity, there's still a lot we don't know, and regardless, nothing we have learned has negated the logical reasoning that Galileo employed centuries ago? Having said this, let's now look at our question of the existence of God from the standpoint of logic.

One of the prime assertions about God is that He created our universe and everything in it. What does science say about the creation of the universe? In the past couple of centuries, our knowledge of this amazing and seemingly endless universe of which we clearly are a part has increased many folds. Technology like the Hubble telescope and sub-atomic physics has greatly increased our understanding of the world we live in. Many existing ideas and assumptions have been examined and clarified scientifically—some rejected, others modified and enlarged, and some even blessed with the label "proven." One thing we did learn is that the universe is expanding at a measurable rate and that if we extrapolate several present known point locations backward in space and time, these extrapolations will converge to a single point, which turns out to be around 13.7 billion years ago. So there is pretty compelling evidence that our universe was somehow formed, created, at that time and place. Now, neither the time nor place is important to our present question, but the fact that the universe somehow did appear at a time and place is vital to the assertion that it did have a creator. An effect must have a cause, and an effect of this magnitude must have a pretty impressive cause.

The scientific community has given the creation of the universe a name. It's called the big bang theory, and though it's not yet a proven fact, it is a theory that has received fairly general acceptance by science. However, even should new data force its modification or even rejection for some more acceptable alternative, the fact of creation and a creator remains unchallenged. Unfortunately, this is about as far as science is going to take us in our quest for proof, but that shouldn't surprise us. Let's look at what the big bang theory is saying. We know that our universe is composed of two primary components, material (which has mass) and energy. We also know that these two components are, under certain conditions, interconvertible. This was dramatically demonstrated in the atomic bomb, in which uranium (material) was converted into massive amounts of energy. The theory postulates that at the time of creation, all the energy and mass that compose the universe were compressed under infinite pressure to form an infinitesimally small "singularity." Instantaneously the restraints were removed, and the singularity began to expand, energy and material together, and have done so ever since. That's a pretty simple-sounding proposal, except when you dwell for a moment on the magnitude of the total material and energy that comprise our universe and then introduce a term like "infinite pressure." Infinity is a concept that is used relatively casually in mathematics, but when you attempt to give it meaning in real life, it becomes almost meaningless. Let's go back for a moment to the total mass of the universe. The earth has a mass of something like ten to the twenty-one set tons.

The sun has 330,000 times the mass of the earth; so the sun, a modest-sized star, has something like a mass of 3×10 to the 26th tons. That's 30,000,000,000,000,000,000,000,000,000 tons. But that's only the start. There are billions of stars in the Milky Way galaxy and billions of galaxies in the universe. A billion is 10^9, so that means something like 3 followed by 48 zeros for the total mass of the universe. That's already a number so huge as to be almost ridiculous. But we have another step in the process of creation. We have to compress that mass to a singularity smaller, much, much smaller than a grain of sand. Now you begin to get some feeling for the magnitude of the creation. It just doesn't seem possible that anyone or anything that we can imagine or visualize in this material world could orchestrate such a process.

Wait a minute. Maybe science just gave us an unintentional boost. With the reason and logic of science, we've eliminated certainly any human being or any material world force as our possible creator. What that leaves is a superbeing, an omniscient and omnipotent being, to deal with these infinity concepts and to plan and execute the creation of our magnificent universe.

Voila!

Not quite so fast. What we've established through science is that our universe was created. How is a theory, a guess if you will, but a guess with some valid scientific thought behind it. Science may even give us some more unexpected help later, but for now, this for me was all that I needed to affirm that my lifetime-conforming belief in Christianity was well placed and sound. It is a scientific fact that our universe was created. Beyond that, it is a sound logical conclusion that the creator was supernatural, God. And since God, why? Why did the omniscient and omnipotent ruler of the spirit world decide to create a material universe? Since we accept God as the creator, He had to exist prior to His creation and also somewhere other than the place that He created. In fact, His new creation must be contained in the same place where He resides. Since we believe that God is spirit, I've elected to call His homeland the spirit world. Back to the question—since God is all-powerful and all-knowing, there is no question that He could perform the creation and maybe for Him it would be a casual act. Maybe one day He was just bored. Maybe some other spirit issued a dare. My innate arrogance compels me to reject such thinking. He had to have a good reason.

The Bible doesn't help us specifically with this question. It just starts with, "In the beginning God created the heavens and the earth," and offers no background for this momentous event. But the more you read the Bible, which is the story of God's interaction with humanity, the more you are exposed to its teachings, the more you are impressed with the obvious fact that God loves His creation and particularly humanity. It seems obvious that all of this was planned and that our relationship with God was an integral and important part of that plan. Again, my arrogance? Why? What other suggestion would seem reasonable? Look again at the Bible. This is God's plan—past, present, and future. Recently I was reading Mark's gospel, and there unquestionably stated is God's plan, that Christ will sacrifice His life for the redemption of humanity's sins and that Christ will come again in the future to claim all believers to eternal life with Him. That's the plan, part of it already achieved, the remainder yet to be accomplished. I'll admit that some of the details of the future are a bit obscure, but the essence of God's plan is there in the Bible for us to see. I'm not surprised at this future confusion since we're dealing with concepts like heaven and eternity, which are clearly beyond the understanding of us humans.

Again, maybe religion's old nemesis, science, has come to our rescue. Recently, I applauded science's gift of the validity of creation, but feared that for all else I must trust to faith alone. But science is full of surprises. The presently most far-reaching and at times most quirky-sounding field of science today is quantum physics. This started in the late nineteenth and early twentieth centuries with studies into the makeup of the atom itself.

Subatomic physics largely was limited to mathematical speculation until the weaponry needs of World War II forced huge expenditures on subatomic research (the atom bomb), which led to research equipment that could test these developed theories. The past fifty to seventy-five years has seen vastly growing interest and research activity in this area. At the same time, cosmology has gone forward in leaps and bounds. Now we have reached the point where meaningful scientific theorizing can delve with reasonable expectation of serious acceptance into areas that formerly were reserved to science fiction. We now seriously can speak of worlds with more dimensions than we are confined to in the four-dimension (three space and time) world in which we live. Cutting-edge theories, "string theory" and "M-theory" require ten and eleven dimensions, respectively. So what's to prevent us now from suggesting that God resides in a different and superior dimension to our world, and this other world is named "spirit world" or "heaven." I don't want to carry these speculations any further at this point, since I have probably already exceeded my bounds in this field of science. It's enough to know that faith could again receive welcome help from science.

It is about time that we review what we have discussed and determine if we have uncovered any compelling arguments in response to our question, "Why believe in God?" or even a step further back, "Does God exist?" For me, science has given us an unquestionable answer to the second of those two questions—at least science compels me to assert that the universe was created at a spot in space and at a specific time. That creation must have had a cause. When you examine what must have been the nature and magnitude of that creation process, as it is described in the big bang theory or will have to be in any modification to or replacement of that theory, you are compelled to discard any "this world" force or cause as being so vastly insufficient as to be disallowed. That compels as an answer either a "supernatural cause" or an ignominious—I just don't know which for a scientist should be embarrassing at least. Thus, our universe was created, but it's creator must have come from another world, a world outside of but encompassing ours. Almost since their creation, humanity has given that cause a name, God. Anything that was beyond human ability or understanding was attributed to God, thunder, lightning, earthquake, and eclipses; even today we call most of these "acts of god." So why change?

Maybe our predecessors were more perceptive than we often give them credit for. This "god" has not always been the caring and loving God of Christianity, but he has always been powerful and all-knowing. If the concept of an omniscient, omnipotent, eternal God is unpalatable to science, how does it turn out that it is science itself that has recently given us a new theory that distinctly provides the possibility of other dimensions in addition to our four-dimensional natural world, of other worlds, of other universes, of a place for God?

Reference

Bible used by Bill in his writings was the NIV Study Bible 10th Anniversary Edition.

About the Author

Marlene Libby was born in a small farming community in western Wisconsin in a Christian home to wonderful Norwegian parents who taught her the importance of loving and caring for others, especially those less fortunate.

She graduated from Amery High School enjoying business courses. Upon graduation, she became employed at a Fortune 500 company in Saint Paul, Minnesota. After taking time off to start a family, she went back to work there in office management and eventually became promoted to sales and marketing manager, traveling the United States, negotiating contracts, and introducing new products. After retiring early, she moved with her husband Bill to Oro

Valley, Arizona, where she enjoyed a successful career in real estate, having many opportunities to share her faith.

Marlene has always been active in the Lutheran church attending youth camps, teaching Sunday school, and holding leadership roles in various organizations. She still loves learning and always has books nearby.

She was fortunate to travel to other countries such as Norway, Italy, Spain, Greece, and Turkey and found it fascinating to visit the locations and learn more about the struggles of the early Christian church.

Although Marlene planned on writing a book on another topic, she placed it on hold to work on this manuscript. This is her first book.

CPSIA information can be obtained
at www.ICGtesting.com
Printed in the USA
BVHW052217151022
649558BV00004B/125